Path

TO THE

Heart

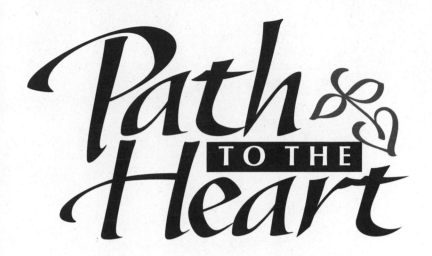

Path TO THE Heart

Informal Talks
On Personal Soul Winning

GLENN A. COON

REVIEW AND HERALD® PUBLISHING ASSOCIATION
HAGERSTOWN, MD 21740

ISBN 0-8280-0784-5

Printed in U.S.A.

Contents

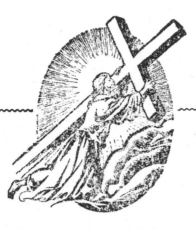

God's Nail

BY MILDRED HILL

Lord, make me a nail upon the wall,
  Fastened securely in its place.
Then from this thing so common and so
    small
  Hang a bright picture of Thy face
That travelers may pause to look
  Upon the loveliness depicted there,
And passing on their weary ways,
  Each radiant face may bear—
Stamped so that nothing can efface—
  The image of Thy glory and Thy grace.
Lord, let not one soul think of me.
Only let me be a nail upon the wall,
  Holding Thy picture in its place.

Introduction

~~~~~~

For the dedicated worker for Christ, there is nothing more essential to his success than the mastery of the science of soul winning until it becomes a divine art. In this book, PATH TO THE HEART, Evangelist Glenn A. Coon draws upon his rich background of public and personal evangelism, to give us these divinely inspired methods of reaching the heart and not merely the head. There are few workers, if any, who have practiced these principles more thoroughly or prepared more carefully to share them.

In this book all who desire to learn the true techniques of soul winning will find the dynamics of Christianity revealed as faith and hope and love blending to make Christians winsome to win some for Christ. Here we have the living proof that "a warm handshake is better than a learned tongue." Here we see the difference between the sounding brass of hard, cold argument, and the soft, enchanting music of the bells of love. Here we breathe the sweet incense of happy witnessing arising from the heated altar of the flaming heart where love has set the life on fire for God. Here we discover why the love of Jesus in the human heart is the greatest fire ever kindled on this earth. From all of these personal case histories and experiences we are led to cry out, Surely "love never faileth."

This book, throbbing with actual experiences of soul winning, proves that the last and best argument for Christianity is a Christian. "A kind, courteous Christian is the most powerful argument that can be produced in favor of Christianity."—*Gospel Workers,* p. 122. PATH TO THE HEART is the finest presentation and application of these divine principles of love in action of anything I have read. I earnestly pray and fervently hope that every Seventh-day Adventist who can read the English language will quickly procure a copy of this timely book and begin at once to practice these principles in his life and in methods of soul winning. The book is fifty years too late. But it is here now! Let us give it a wide circulation and thus help to redeem the time. Here is a book that should be—not only in every Seventh-day Adventist library—it should be in every Christian heart. Let us saturate our minds with these beautiful methods of reaching human hearts. "The world needs today what it needed nineteen hundred years ago—a revelation of Christ."—*The Ministry of Healing,* p. 143. Here at last, is a book showing how this is done.

ADLAI ALBERT ESTEB, PH.D.
Editor, *GO: The Journal for
Adventist Laymen*

"Jesus Only"

~~~~~~

*P*ROF. ALBERT EINSTEIN was once asked, "If you were to live your life over again, what would you choose to be?"

His answer was, "I would not be a scientist, a scholar, or a teacher. I would be a plumber or a peddler." What an evaluation of our scientific age with its modern discoveries, including the death-dealing A-bomb!

But the discovery, the secret, which I wish to share with you here has brought, not death and destruction, but life and harmony to untold millions. The secret was discovered more than nineteen hundred years ago on a "high mountain apart" in the land of Palestine (Matt. 17:1). It was at the scene of the glorious transfiguration, when three men "saw no man any more" (Mark 9:8). Luke pictures the discovery of that long-to-be-remembered event in these words, "Jesus was found alone" (Luke 9:36). The discovery was made "when they had lifted up their eyes" (Matt. 17:8). The secret formula of power was "Jesus only."

GREATEST DISCOVERY

"Jesus only" is the greatest discovery of all time. It is even greater than the secret of the A-bomb. Even the

enemies of the cause of Christ declared that these men had
"turned the world upside down" (Acts 17:6). More po-
tent than the hydrogen bomb, this secret melts hard hearts
of all who lift up their eyes above the sins and weaknesses
of neighbors, church members, or relatives, to Jesus Christ
of Nazareth, the Saviour of the world.

With the discovery of the A-bomb formula, our Government put forth every effort to keep it secret, but
traitors sold out for money. The secret discovered on the
Mount of Transfiguration, which "they kept . . . close, and
told no man in those days" (Luke 9:36), was, soon after
Calvary's tragedy, revealed to the entire then-known world.
And it was because of their sheer love of it, and the pure
joy of sharing this wonderful Name with such heavenly
power, that these three men heralded to the world their
great discovery, their close secret.

For awhile Peter refused to share it. During the trial of
Jesus before Annas and Caiaphas, Peter denied that Name.
When the damsel suggested that he must be acquainted
with Jesus of Nazareth, he told her, in effect, that he had
never so much as heard that Name (Matt. 26:69, 70). In
a few moments he denied it again, this time with an oath.
And some time later that same night he covered the pre-
ciousness of that wonderful Name with the cloak of profanity (Matt. 26:74).

COVERED WITH COMMONNESS

That powerful Name has often since that time been
covered with commonness. During college days I met a
young man whose home was only about eight miles from
the famous Niagara Falls. He had heard about Niagara
Falls so much that the name had become common to him.
Its charm and wonder, which attracted people by the
thousands from all parts of America, and the world, meant

little to him. That famed name that awakened awe in the hearts of thousands, to him was lost in the common speech of his friends and neighbors.

So today the name of Jesus is used in jest and in joke, in profanity and obscenity. It is heard from the mouth of the vulgar, the drunkard, and the infidel. Today that Name is not commonly appreciated for what it truly is. "Thou shalt call his name JESUS: for he shall save his people from their sins" (Matt. 1:21).

As Peter witnessed the character of Jesus under suffering, persecution, and insult, he began to see the meaning of that wonderful Name. The transfiguration scene must have come up before him again and again during the trial that Thursday night. He remembered the words from heaven he had heard, "This is my beloved Son, in whom I am well pleased; hear ye him" (Matt. 17:5). Jesus stood uncondemned before Pilate—only an earthly governor—yet Christ was "King of kings, and Lord of lords" in character.

Peter also saw Him move, without a murmur, toward Calvary, carrying the heavy cross. And on Golgotha's height he heard Jesus utter a prayer of forgiveness for His enemies. Then, and then only, did Peter begin to understand, in even a small measure, the beauty and power that is wrapped up in that Name.

POWER OF PENTECOST

"Jesus only" was the power of Pentecost when three thousand were converted in a day (Acts 2:41). Those three thousand men and women, and more, were spellbound, not by Peter's words merely, but by Peter—changed Peter. He was transformed by "Jesus only." He was regenerated by that look of pity cast upon him by the Saviour in the judgment hall. The multitudes felt that a

Name that could change a denier into an orator for the cross of Christ was a Name *they* needed. Crying out, "Men and brethren, what shall we do?" the great crowd of convicted hearers were told to "repent, and be baptized" in that wonderful Name. It had truly baptized Peter's very life, his soul, his all.

In gladness three thousand souls were led into the baptismal waters by the ministers of Pentecost (Acts 2:37, 38, 41, 46). They had learned the secret of the life and power found in "Jesus only." This secret, which they had kept close in those days, was now being heralded to the entire world of their generation. "They were of 'one accord,' 'of one heart and of one soul.' Christ filled their thoughts; the advancement of His kingdom was their aim. In mind and character they had become like their Master." —*The Acts of the Apostles*, p. 45. They had become *like* Him. That is why they could preach Him.

A few days after Pentecost it was the power of Jesus' name that gave "perfect soundness" to the cripple who sat at the gate called Beautiful. Peter and John were about to enter the Temple at the hour of prayer, when the lame man stopped them and asked alms of them. Peter had no silver or gold, but he did have a *Name*. And there was healing in that Name. "In the name of Jesus Christ of Nazareth rise up and walk," Peter cries, and lifts him by his right hand. The man leaps for joy and follows Peter and John right on into the Temple. Crowds look on, and begin to run toward this man who is holding on to Peter and John in delighted wonderment. But Peter cries out and tells them about Jesus. "His name through faith in his name hath made this man strong" (Acts 3:1-16). Peter preached Christ because he had become like Him.

When I was beginning my ministry I came across a little book that presented the name of Jesus very simply and most attractively. It showed the power that is in that Name. I was thrilled as I had never been, perhaps, since my mother first painted for me a picture of Jesus while she was sweeping my room, when I was about six years of age. The wonderful picture mother had painted for me then, came back with renewed beauty in the pages of that little book. I fell in love with Jesus all over again in a very special way. I knelt before God and asked Him to help me to present Jesus to others in all His loveliness.

It was not long afterward that I was privileged to do so in my limited way. I was called to conduct a special short series of meetings. As I presented Jesus in His power and loveliness, I felt the angels of heaven clustering around me. My heart was warmed by the presence of Jesus. I could note the same spirit and response on the part of the audience as well.

During that week people were released from the power of sin, just as the impotent man at the Beautiful Gate of the Temple was released from physical infirmity. Crippled souls were restored. Critical spirits were freed from the prison house of sin. Gossiping Christians turned to Christ for victory. Hearts filled with vice were cleansed and became the habitation of Jesus, the Saviour of the world.

THE CONFESSION

In a testimony service one morning during that week, a young man told of how he had been reared in a most critical home. His father had evidently never been in that "high mountain apart," where people "see no man any more." He had made people—not Jesus—the subject of his conversation. People were the object of his criticism. People's weaknesses were the topic of his discussion. So this young man's spiritual growth was stunted by the blighting atmosphere of criticism.

13

This Christless spirit of criticism stunts the growth of anyone. The boy needed Jesus. But Jesus was not found in that professedly Christian home. He was not found in their judgment of others. He was not found in their words of denunciation. He was not found as they looked at sinners in the church, or hypocrites in religion. All this became so distasteful to the young lad that he decided religion was not for him. He went out into the world, trying to satisfy the craving of his heart. But the world cannot satisfy. Its soap-bubble pleasures soon burst. Then he lapsed into a state of utter discouragement. Life became one long nightmare. "Every time," he said, speaking of this horrible experience, "I saw a funeral procession moving down the street, I wished I were in that box." He pictured his sorrow, his pain, his lost condition, in a home where Christ was professed but not possessed.

Then suddenly his eyes brightened as he exclaimed with joy, "But this week I have found Jesus." He tried to describe the great happiness that was now his. But his lips could not utter it. His speech was inadequate to tell it. His tongue could not frame it. But his experience was the same as that of those three men on the "high mountain apart" when "Jesus was found alone."

To me this young man is a symbol of many today who are searching for the secret of satisfaction. They are lonesome for Jesus, but they know it not. They are thirsty for the water of life, but do not recognize it. Christ is that living water. Jesus only satisfies. Every doctrine we have to present to the world is a doctrine about Jesus. And when we do not present it as a doctrine concerning Jesus, we do not present it as we should. To divest doctrine of Jesus Christ is to take from it its life, its impetus, its challenge, its motivating power. Jesus is the answer to the cravings of the soul. For "in thy presence is fulness of joy;

at thy right hand there are pleasures for evermore" (Ps. 16:11).

The impotent man at the gate called Beautiful reminds me of another man who for more than forty years had also been crippled. His was not physical but spiritual deformity. But now he was dying—dying not far from the church of which he had been a member for more than forty years. He was not ready to die; for he too had been living in an atmosphere of criticism. He had judged others. He had condemned. The objects of his attacks were his neighbors, church members, teachers, ministers. What he needed to do was to go up to a "high mountain apart" where he could lift up his eyes above the failures and follies of so-called Christians, and "behold the Lamb of God, which taketh away the sin of the world" (John 1:29). He needed to follow the Saviour's instruction, "Look unto me, and be ye saved" (Isa. 45:22). For by "beholding" we become "changed" (2 Cor. 3:18).

A doctor neighbor of his came to see me. "Brother Coon," he said, "would you be willing to go over and pray with this neighbor of mine? I am afraid to have him die in his present condition. Perhaps you can do something for him."

"I shall be happy to do so," I replied.

Taking with me a young minister and the good Christian doctor, I went to see the poor old gentleman. As we rode to his home I asked the Lord to help me to cause the dying man to lift up his eyes and see "Jesus only."

As we stepped into this poor man's bedroom I said, "Rejoice, brother! We have come to bring you hope. We have come to bring you Jesus."

Instantly his eyes filled with tears. His voice choked with emotion. "Brother, I can't find Him any more! I can't find Him any more!" was his pitiful reply.

15

"I will tell you how to find Jesus again," I comfortingly replied. And I opened my Bible right there on his bed. "I will show you how to find Jesus," I continued. And the text I used you can use. I turned to 1 John 1:9: "If we confess our sins, he is faithful and just to forgive us our sins, and to cleanse us from all unrighteousness." Then I turned to Isaiah 45:22. This is a beautiful verse. And so simple. "Look unto me, and be ye saved."

"Now," I said, "we are kneeling right down by your bedside and we are going to confess our sins. You are going to confess your sins too. And as you confess your sins, tell the Lord that you believe, for Jesus' sake, that He *has* forgiven and *has* cleansed you." That is *very* important. Peter declared that it was "faith in his name" that gave the crippled man "perfect soundness." So this poor dying man, with his crippled soul, was to receive "perfect soundness" only by "faith in his name."

"Now," I said, "you are looking to Jesus; looking to Him as the one who forgives and cleanses you." And then we prayed.

"I BELIEVE!"

When we had finished our prayer, he prayed. As he prayed, his voice choked again. He asked God to forgive him for his past neglect, his sins and his mistakes. He did not talk any more about the mistakes of his brethren in the church. He did not speak of the mistakes of the teachers in the school. He did not think about the mistakes of anyone else—only his own. He asked God to forgive him for his *own* mistakes.

But he could not get "I believe" in his prayer. You know, it is amazing how hard it is to be simple, isn't it? He just could not get in that expression of faith, "Lord, I believe."

16

And so I said, "Brother, now before we rise, just tell the Lord, 'I believe.'"

You know, Hebrews 4:2 says that the people who left Egypt never got into the Promised Land—none but two—because they did not *mix* the promise with faith.

"Now, brother," I said, "say, 'Lord, I believe.'"

And it seemed that from the very inner soul of that poor dying man came the words, "I believe!"

"O brother," I said, "that is wonderful! Can you tell the Lord that again? Tell Him again that you believe, for that connects you with God."

And again he repeated, *"I believe!"*

FOUND JESUS

As we rose I said, "Brother, now you have found Jesus. You know that He has forgiven your sins, don't you? He has cleansed you. Now you are looking to Him, aren't you?"

He replied, "Yes, I am." And tears were in his eyes.

"Now," I asked him, "just before we leave, won't you tell the Lord and us once again that you believe He has done this for you? You believe you are His child? Can you say again, 'I believe'?"

He looked me full in the face, and from the depths of his soul exclaimed with solemn, holy joy that must have charmed the angels around the throne, "I *believe!*" And God forgave and cleansed him right there!

"Now you are a child of God," I assured him. "When the devil comes to you again, you just say, 'Christ has cleansed me. He has forgiven me. I am looking to Jesus. I am now His child. I am being saved by His power.'"

As we left that home there was a glow of certainty in that dear man's face. He had been made a child of God by faith in Christ. I was happy that I had presented Jesus, the Saviour of the world, to that poor man, so near the end of

2

life's journey. I was delighted that he had lifted up his eyes on a "high mountain apart," where he could see "no man any more, save Jesus only."

A few days later I learned that the dear old man had passed away. But I believe with all my heart I shall see him on the glorious resurrection morning, when Jesus calls to life those who have found salvation in Jesus on the "high mountain apart."

Now, friend, *you* can do that. You really can. There are many of us, perhaps, who could not be too deep, or too theological. But when it is just a question of using two or three simple texts of Scripture, and helping a person to reach up his hand of faith and get it into the hand of Jesus, *you* can do that. And then you can tell the sinner that Jesus keeps His Word. Oh, that gives a man hope! Then he looks to Jesus. That is salvation.

As I have meditated upon this experience I have prayed, "Lord, forgive me wherein I have tried to get beyond the simplicity of Jesus." "Thou shalt call his name JESUS: for he shall save his people from their sins" (Matt. 1:21).

POWERFUL NAME

After Peter was used of God to bring that healing Name to the cripple, he was brought, with John, before the same Annas and Caiaphas (Acts 4:6-12) who had just a few weeks earlier sat in judgment on Christ (Matt. 26:57, 58). When Jesus was tried, Peter had denied the Name. Peter's persecutors doubtless thought he would certainly do so again, especially if they reconstructed the scene as nearly as possible like the one in which Peter had before become frightened and denied his Lord.

This was on the very next day after the healing of the cripple. "And it came to pass on the morrow, that their rulers, and elders, and scribes, and Annas the high priest, and Caiaphas, and John, and Alexander, and as many as were of the kindred of the high priest, were gathered together at Jerusalem" (Acts 4:5, 6). I can see even the maid—the damsel who six weeks before accused Peter of belonging to Jesus—sitting there too. Her eyes meet his. But this time there is no sign of fright or timidity in Peter's eyes, heart, or voice.

You will have to read the rest of the record for yourself to see what the name of Jesus had done to the vacillating Peter. It thrills my heart! As Peter tells about "the name of Jesus" (Acts 4:10), I see Annas move nervously, and Caiaphas turn to one side as if to be shielded from the sharp arrow of conviction. The maid turns pale. She can scarcely believe her very eyes! What has happened to this profane denier of but a few short weeks before? They are inquiring of their own hearts. Ah, he has been converted and saved. He answers their unspoken question: "Neither is there salvation in any other: for there is none other name under heaven given among men, whereby we must be saved" (Acts 4:12). Peter preached Christ because he loved Him and had become like Him.

I wonder whether Saul of Tarsus was there too when Peter so beautifully testified to the name of Jesus. Later when the great persecutor had become a champion of the faith of Jesus he exclaimed, "Wherefore God also hath highly exalted him, and given him a name which is above every name" (Phil. 2:9).

" 'Jesus only'—in these words is contained the secret of the life and power that marked the history of the early church."—*The Acts of the Apostles,* p. 64. And since God is no respecter of persons, that same Name is the secret of the life and power of every man or woman, boy or girl, who will come up into the "high mountain apart," to an experience where he sees "no man any more," but where "Jesus was found alone" two thousand years ago, and will again be found of all who sincerely seek Him.

PREACH CHRIST IN DOCTRINE

I believe that the more we become like Christ, the more we shall love to preach *Him* in all doctrine. And the more we preach Him in sincerity, the more we should love Him. Jesus stated, "And this is life eternal, that they might know thee the only true God, and Jesus Christ, whom thou hast sent" (John 17:3). Since all life is centered in Jesus, it follows that all doctrine should be Christ centered. He is "the way, the truth, and the life" (John 14:6). Therefore, we must "say the truth *in* Christ" (Rom 9:1). All spiritual truth should be "truth *of* Christ" (2 Cor. 11:10), and "truth *in* Christ" (1 Tim. 2:7).

Some time ago a medical doctor invited me to visit a patient of his with him. He said she had tuned in to some of the broadcasts by a very good evangelist who had recently been in that city. He added, "Maybe we can do something for her."

We cannot expect to do very much for a person, doctrinally, the first time we meet him. That is where we sometimes make a great mistake. We try to give too much doctrine too soon. And yet I did not want to disappoint the doctor. So I asked the Lord to help me to uplift Jesus.

After we were nicely seated in this woman's home she began, "I have listened to a lot of your broadcasts, but I don't believe in that Sabbath question, and I don't believe in hell as you teach it."

"Oh," I replied, "is that all you don't believe? That is wonderful! So you believe everything but that? That is wonderful!"

20

Do you know what that did to her heart? It helped to open it. When we start arguing, that closes the heart. So I did not argue. I agreed with her all I could. I tried to be as *kind as* Jesus as I talked *about* Jesus. Sometimes we Christians become too dogmatic, you know.

"Now," she continued, "tell me something about this hell business."

"Well," I answered her, "to properly understand the subject of hell, we must study it in the light of the character of Jesus. You see, 'This is life eternal, that they might know thee the only true God, and Jesus Christ, whom thou hast sent' (John 17:3). Therefore it is impossible for any man to properly understand the subject of the punishment of the wicked except as he studies it in the light of the character of Jesus."

And I determined that I would not argue. You see, that is a bad thing to do. That is not the spirit of Jesus. We must just l-o-v-e them into Jesus. Soul winning is a love affair.

And so I continued, "Did you hear just the other day about those two boys who caught another boy who was guilty of a misdemeanor and tortured him for hours?"

"No," she exclaimed. "Shame on them! Inhuman of them! That's inhuman!"

I could see that she had protested so much that I would have to be careful how I applied the incident. If I should make the application too quickly, she might be embarrassed. That is not Jesus' method. So I asked the Lord to help me not to say anything that would hurt her.

And so I continued very slowly and thoughtfully, "Now we are thinking about Jesus and the subject of hell-fire. You know, 'we love him because he first loved us,' don't we?"

"Yes," she agreed, "indeed we do. He is wonderful!"

"You are right," I replied. And I tried to keep on her

21

side of the argument as much as possible. That way she would not be embarrassed. "Jesus is *so* wonderful and loving! Just because I refused to serve Him, would He torture me throughout eternity? Now I am not trying to put you in the corner. But it *is* something to think about, isn't it?" And I saw by her eyes that she had caught the point.

"Yes," she said, "but people have the power of choice."

"Yes, so did that boy who committed the misdemeanor," I replied. "And just because I have the power of choice, if I *choose* not to serve Jesus, He still will not torture me. He loves His enemies. That is what He taught us to do—'love your enemies.' So Jesus loves His enemies." And then I explained to her a few texts on hell-fire.

Changing the subject, she said, "By the way, what do you teach regarding eternal security—once saved, always saved?"

"Well," I replied, "you see——"

And I watched to see that there was no "heat" in my voice or my look. You know, sometimes we generate more heat than light in our discussions. And when heat is generated, usually the light grows dim. It does not do a bit of good to argue with one whom we are seeking to enlighten, because we are not representing Jesus when we are generating heat in an argument.

So I said, "You see, in order to understand eternal security, we must study it in the light of the character of Jesus. That is the secret of understanding all the doctrines of the Bible. Every doctrine is given us to help us to love Jesus more and to understand Him better. Now, what is the fundamental law of Jesus? Is it not the law of love?"

"Yes, it is," she agreed.

"And now," I added, "can we love without the power of choice?"

"No," was her response.

"The law of love and the power of choice are the fundamental laws of Jesus, aren't they?"

"Yes," she assented.

"Now," I continued, "you take the sinner. Will Jesus compel that sinner to serve Him?"

"No," she replied.

"Why? Because Jesus wants that man to serve Him because he loves Him. He must *choose* for himself. So Christ does not compel him *before* he becomes a Christian. He does not *compel* him to be a Christian, does He? 'Choose you this day whom ye will serve.' 'We love him, because he first loved us.' Now, that is when he is still a sinner. Jesus does not compel him, does he?"

"No," she said, "I should say *not.*"

"Now," I went on, "*after* that man becomes a *saint,* does Jesus *compel* him to remain a *saint?*"

"Oh no," was her reply.

"You are right. When the sinner becomes a saint, Jesus still does not *compel* him to *remain* a saint. If he *chooses,* he can give up Jesus, can't he?" I queried.

And I could see just then that it clicked. When it *clicked,* I did not argue. We must be careful not to use too many proofs in trying to make a point. Why? Because it might embarrass an individual. He might get the impression that we think he is below par mentally, or that we think we are superior. So we should not use so many proofs that *it forces* the argument. It might cause him to feel that we think *we* are intelligent and *he* is not. So you see, when I saw that she caught the point, I did not go any further. I did not argue at all. We covered other doctrines. But each time I presented Jesus to her in the doctrine. And I saw she did not refuse the doctrine, because she loved Jesus.

Finally I said, "We must be going. But before we do so, we want to pray for your health. We understand you are not too well physically. We want to ask Jesus, who healed the sick nineteen centuries ago, to put His hand of healing upon you."

"Oh, thank you so much," she said gratefully.

And as we knelt to pray I said, "Doctor, will you lead us in prayer?"

The doctor prayed a beautiful prayer. In his prayer he said, "Lord, this afternoon as I have sat here I have learned something as Brother Coon has been studying with us." What was the doctor doing? He was humbling himself, putting himself in the same class as a learner with the woman whom we were trying to help.

What did that statement of his help this woman to do? It helped her to accept what we were saying, because we were carrying to her not merely *doctrines* of Jesus but the *spirit* of Jesus as well. And she did not feel at any time that there was a gulf between us. We must always remember that we are not merely to *talk about* Jesus, but we are to *have Jesus* in our hearts. That is what counts. "If any man have not the Spirit of Christ, he is none of his," the Scripture states (Rom. 8:9). "A legal religion can never lead souls to Christ; for it is a loveless, Christless religion."— *The Desire of Ages*, p. 280.

Let us look for Jesus every time we study the Bible. We should never be content to find abstract doctrine, but rather Jesus *in* doctrine. I make it a practice always in my personal study to ask myself the question, "What does this study do to my understanding of Jesus? What lesson concerning Him does it bring to me?" When I have found Jesus there, I have found light and life.

Several years ago I received a one-hundred-ten-page, handwritten letter from a woman I had never met. It contained many Bible quotations. There was nothing personally from the author except a note requesting my analysis of the long, long letter.

Asking the Lord to help me to read with an open mind, ready to receive any message He might have for me, if it was there, I began to read. There was page after page of Bible warnings and threatenings from the Lord. It quoted Scriptures of coming gloom and darkness, of war and tempest, of sorrow and death. But it offered no hope.

In my reply to the author I stated that I believed all the scriptural quotations were correct, but that I noticed she had *lifted* from the context warnings, pictures of darkness, pictures of gloom, threatened judgments. But just before her quotation of that threatened judgment was a beautiful picture of Jesus. Or just *after* it was a glorious message of hope. But she had left that out. The threatenings and warnings were there, but no Jesus—the only One who can save from the threatening gloom and darkness.

Thus the long, long letter, all the way through, spoke of fear and gloom, despair and discouragement. And the Lord was left out. The Light of the world was missing. The only hope of humanity was not to be found there.

I concluded that the author of this letter felt called of God to give the Laodicean message of Revelation 3. So I had to tell the author that I must believe that the Lord of Revelation 3:20 was evidently standing on the outside of the door of that letter, pleading for entrance. The author had not let Him in.

Then as I thought it over I wondered whether He had not stood on the outside of the door of some of my sermons, my conversation, my life at times, pleading, gently and patiently, for admission. It is a serious thing to keep the Author of life and joy *outside* our lives. Oh, we should let Him in!

Jesus promised His church, "Lo, I am with you alway" (Matt. 28:20). This was a very real promise to them. Like Moses, the early church endured "as seeing him who is invisible" (Heb. 11:27). "Moses did not merely think of God, he saw Him. . . . Never did he lose sight of His face." —*Education*, p. 63.

"When the disciples first heard the words of Christ, they felt their need of Him. They sought, they found, they followed Him. They were with Him in the temple, at the table, on the mountain-side, in the field. . . . After the Saviour's ascension, the sense of the divine presence, full of love and light, was still with them. It was a *personal* presence."—*The Acts of the Apostles*, pp. 64, 65.

OPEN THE DOOR

I have felt for a long time that we should practice the presence of Jesus more than we do. Many years ago I read of an eminent Christian who set an extra plate at his table, occasionally, for Jesus as his guest—not that Christ needed it or would eat from the plate, but that act helped him to be more conscious of the presence of Jesus. And I often thought, "Isn't that interesting!" However, it seemed a little unnecessary to me. And it *is* unnecessary. But I found that I was not conscious enough, even as a minister, of the presence of Jesus. And it bothered me.

One day I was traveling alone, by car, to conduct a series of revival meetings some distance from our home. I drove out of the city a short distance and stopped the car. I thought, "If that Christian of whom I read could invite Jesus to sit at his table, and even set an extra plate for Him, why can't I invite Jesus to ride with me in the car? Has He not said, 'Lo, I am with you alway'? The fact that I am asking Him to ride with me will cause me to be conscious of His presence."

So I stepped out of the car, walked around it, opened the right front door, and invited Jesus to be my guest and ride with me. I closed the door, stepped back around the car, opened my door, sat under the wheel, and drove on. And I talked with Jesus. I do not know when I have ever been more conscious of His presence. I *felt* Him there. I had opened the door.

It was not my intention to mention this experience to anyone. But at one of those revival services I did refer to it. I told how Jesus had been more real to me by that little act of my opening the door, by my own choice.

A few days later I was visiting in a home. The woman said to me, "Brother Coon, I have had a very happy day. I went home that night after you mentioned about your inviting Jesus to ride with you. The next morning when my children had gone to school and my husband to work, I said to myself: 'If Brother Coon can invite Jesus to ride with him in the car, why can't I invite Jesus to be with me in my home today?' So I stepped to the front door. And as I opened it, I said, 'Jesus, will You be my guest today?' And, Brother Coon," she said joyfully, "I have never been happier in all my life than today." She had opened the door to Jesus. It was her own choice.

It is good to do things like that. Not that they in themselves are so important. But it is good to do things that will help us to be more conscious of the presence of Jesus.

I was relating that experience in a church recently. There was a woman there who had a little girl about six years of age who was causing her trouble. She would wander around the neighborhood with children who did not know the Lord. They were teaching her bad habits. She would then return home and be saucy to her mother. The mother's heart was just about breaking.

The mother thought to herself, "I wonder if maybe

setting a place at the table for Jesus today would help my little girl to be less saucy."

So she said to the child, "We are going to set the table now. And we are going to set a place for Jesus." I had told them that occasionally we do that in our home. "And we are going to put on the prettiest plate and glass, and set up a chair."

All interest, the little girl asked, "Mommy, will Jesus *really* be here?"

"Yes, Jesus will be right in this room," mother replied.

"But," persisted the little girl, "will Jesus be right in that chair, Mommy?"

"Jesus will be with us just as though we could *see* Him in that chair," returned the mother.

The little girl looked on in wonderment. After the table was spread, they sat down.

Mother said, "Now we are going to ask Jesus to bless the food."

They closed their eyes and asked Jesus' blessing upon the food. In relating the experience to us, the mother said, "As we were eating, my little daughter sat there as though she was sitting in the presence of royalty." And she was, wasn't she?

And all at once the little girl forgot the plate, and the place that had been set for Jesus. So she reverted to her old ways. "Mommy, you think you're smart, don't you?" began the child.

"Then I looked in the direction of the place that I had set for Jesus," the mother said as she was relating the experience to us. "Very quietly I said, 'Jesus, I don't think that was very nice. Do you?'"

Instantly the little girl did what she would have done could she have seen Jesus sitting there. She reached over and patted her mother on the wrist, all embarrassed, just as though she could see Jesus. And she said, "Now, Mommy, you know I really didn't mean that. Now, Mommy, I really didn't mean that."

The loving Saviour stands at the door of our hearts, pleading, so tenderly, "Behold, I stand at the door, and knock: if any man hear my voice, and open the door, I will come in to him, and will sup with him" (Rev. 3:20).

Let us take Jesus into our lives. Let us invite Him to be with us at our tables. Let us take Him into our thinking. Let us take Him with us everywhere we go, and make Him a part of whatever we do. Then let us preach Him in doctrine. Let us not tack Him on as a postscript. But let Jesus leaven *all* our teaching, *all* our preaching, *all* our Bible studies, and *all* our conversation. Let Him be to us, as He was to Moses, a *personal presence*. And then let us never rest satisfied until we become *like* Him. Then someday soon, with purest joy, we shall see Him face to face.

THE WAY HOME

A little girl was lost in the great city of London. Finding the little one in this sad plight, the police tried to help her.

"What is your name?"

"Patsy."

"Patsy—what?"

"I don't know."

"What's your daddy's name?"

"I don't know," wailed the child.

"Where do you live?"

"I don't know," was all they could get for a reply. The poor little tot was too frightened, confused, and bewildered to give them any information.

The police pointed out one building after another, hoping they might mention something she would recognize as being near her home. But there was no response from the frightened child. The various places and objects they mentioned meant nothing to her.

"What shall we do?" they questioned.

Then one of the officers thought of the giant cross on top of one of London's great cathedrals. "Do you know the *big* cross on top of the cathedral?" he asked.

At this the little girl's eyes brightened. "Yes. Oh yes!" she exclaimed. "Take me to the cross. I can find my way home from there!"

There are confused, frustrated, lost children of God all over this old world. They are trying to find a marker that will show them the way home. Condemnation will only make them all the more confused. Argument, good as it is, is insufficient. Logic, as important as it is, is not enough. Abstract Bible doctrine will not accomplish it.

But the likeness of Jesus in our lives, in our teaching, in our conversation, in our consciousness, will be a marker for weary, lost souls. With the wonderful truths of the Scriptures, as they are in Christ, people can find their way home to the Father's house.

"Jesus only" is the secret of the life and power that must mark the history of the church today if we would fulfill our mission. But in order to find Him, let us go up into a "high mountain apart." There we shall see "no man any more." But where "Jesus was found alone" on the Mount of Transfiguration nineteen hundred years ago, He may be found of all today. But we must first lift up our eyes from the valleys of human weakness, human hypocrisy, human failure, to the wonderful Christ, who has a name that is above every name. If we do this, we too may expect many to stop in their mad course of selfishness to see "no man any more, save Jesus only."

Enamored With Jesus

H IS MOUTH is most sweet: yea, he is altogether lovely. This is my beloved, and this is my friend" (Song of Sol. 5:16).

"FRIEND"

A little boy was in a house of refuge. In a class recitation one day he was asked to spell the word "friend." He paused and studied a moment, and then slowly from his lips came the letters "f-r-i-e-n-d." When asked what was the meaning of the word "friend," he thought another instant. Then he said, "It is a feller who knows all about ye and loves ye just the same."

That is Jesus. "And *this* is my friend."

A poison arrow had wounded Edward I of England. Immediately his wife Eleanor put her mouth to the wound, and at the risk of her own life, drew out the poison that would have taken his life.

Six thousand years ago the poison arrows of sin had wounded the human race. But Jesus rushed to our rescue, extracting the virus of sin from all who would let Him. But He did it at the cost of His own life; for He died in awful agony on Calvary's tree—"the Lamb slain from the foundation of the world" (Rev. 13:8).

"ALTOGETHER LOVELY"

"Mamma," spoke up a little girl as mother was tucking the quilts around her for the night, "what makes your hand look so ugly and twisted? It doesn't look like other people's."

"You see, honey," mother tenderly replied, "when you were younger than you are now, a fire broke out in the room where you were sleeping. I hurried upstairs to put out the fire, but your night clothes had already caught on fire. In tearing the flaming clothes from your body, my hand was severely burned and twisted, so that it does not look much like a hand any more. But, darling, I was able to save your life."

From that moment on, that scarred, twisted hand of her mother's was probably the most beautiful hand that child ever beheld.

Long centuries ago we were doomed to die. And Jesus just could not stand it to be in heaven while we perished. So He hurried down to earth to save us at any cost. In the thick of the battle to save us, His brow was pierced again and again by long Palestine thorns. His back was lacerated and the blood spurted out. His side was cut open by a spear thrust. And His very hands and feet were cut through with crucifixion nails. As He hung on the cross that sultry Friday afternoon, His closest relatives and friends scarcely recognized Him—His features were so changed, His body so mutilated.

But throughout eternity, for those of us who get there, heaven's greatest beauty will be the glorified scars of Jesus. For "he is altogether lovely. This is my beloved, and this is my friend" (Song of Sol. 5:16).

A New Convert

Many years ago I had the privilege of baptizing a man who had great zeal for the church he was entering. He believed he could win perhaps five thousand souls in a single year. I was of course accustomed to witnessing such zeal in new believers. And I would not for a moment discourage him. He went on to say, "When I am baptized the church will be full of just my friends alone." But to his great disappointment only three lone friends came to witness his baptism. In a short time he himself had given up his new faith.

Why was this? I believe the new convert used wrong methods. He had zeal but not knowledge. There are doubtless many others today who are still in the church but have had a similarly disappointing experience. They were once enthusiastic, but now they are discouraged. They have tried to win souls, but have miserably failed. Some will give up entirely, thinking soul winning is not for them. Some are ready to try new methods. But others will still struggle on, using the same old, unsuccessful methods year after year. They bring no one to Christ, yet it never dawns on them to change their methods.

The Poultryman

Let us say that Mr. Smith is a poultryman. I am introduced to him. In the conversation that follows I inquire: "What is your occupation, Mr. Smith?"

"Oh, I am a poultryman," he replies.

"That is fine," I respond. "How long have you followed this occupation?"

"About ten years."

Very much interested in his success, I inquire, "About how many chickens do you raise a year, Mr. Smith?"

After a moment's hesitation he replies, "With what I expect to raise this year, I will have my first chicken."

I am sure I must have misunderstood Mr. Smith. So I carefully repeat a number of my questions to be sure we understand each other. Yes, I heard him rightly. He is a poultryman—has been for ten years. He specializes in raising chickens. And yet, after ten years of labor, he has not succeeded in raising a single chicken!

You know without my telling you what I would be thinking. Yes, I would say to myself, "If Mr. Smith intends ever to succeed in raising chickens, he had better try some other method." Isn't that right?

And yet there are Christians who go year after year without winning a soul to Christ. They think the reason for their failure is merely that the world is hard. They have urged and nagged and scolded. They have condemned and denounced and criticized. But it has never dawned on them that they had better change their methods if they are to be successful in leading a friend, a relative, a neighbor, to their wonderful Lord.

Some Christians try to make the choice for others. They do not realize that the decision to accept or reject Christ is a personal, individual matter. And since each man must make his own decision, the part of the Christian is to present Christ in such an attractive manner that their friends will, of their own volition, *choose* Him as their Lord and Saviour.

"LEARN OF ME"

Let us examine for a few moments the two methods, or philosophies, of soul winning. First notice with me Christ's method. Jesus bids us, "Learn of me" (Matt. 11:29). And Jesus says, "I will allure her" (Hosea 2:14). "I will *allure* her, . . . and speak comfortably unto her." (Margin: "to her heart," or, "friendly.")

Jesus is here speaking of a wanderer who has gone so far from God that such a one is likened to Gomer, the wife of Hosea. Hosea's wife was unfaithful to him. She connected herself with an ordinary paramour. Finally even he became so disgusted with her that he sold her on the common slave market. And, bless your heart, who do you suppose went down to the slave market to purchase her? —Hosea, her former husband. Can you imagine that?

The account is penned for our learning and instruction that we might know the method of winning a soul to Christ. Hosea represented God and His love for His backslidden, wandering people. "I will allure her." Allure whom? That defiled, unfaithful, unworthy, ungrateful wretch!

If you or I had gone out to bring back such a one, *we* might have said, "I will scold her. I'll let her know the awful thing she has done. Maybe it will bring her to her senses."

But no, God said, "I will *allure* her." Which is the right method?

We might have said, "I will go down and give it to her straight from the shoulder." But God said, "I will give her My love straight from My heart." "I will *allure* her . . . and speak to her heart" (Hosea 2:14, margin). Which is the better method?

We might have boasted, "I'll tell you, I didn't mince matters with her. I told her in no uncertain terms that she was a filthy sinner. I looked her straight in the eye—and she knew I meant business—and said to her, 'Why don't you straighten up and behave yourself?'" And then doubtless we would have reported it as "one missionary visit." But the devil would say, "*That* visit belongs in *my* book. That was a visit for me." And it would have been, wouldn't it?

35

CHRIST'S METHOD

But God shows the way to win her back again. Loathsome though her character may be, He declares, "I will allure her." That is God's philosophy of soul winning. Ellen G. White, speaking of Jesus and His method, sums it up like this: "His blessings He presents in the most *alluring* terms."—*The Desire of Ages,* p. 826.

I used to think that word "allure" belonged to the devil. Really I did. I was brought up to believe that any use of the word "allure" was always connected with some form of immorality. I did not know that the word "allure" belongs in the vocabulary of God and Christ. But there we find it in the book of Hosea.

"His blessings He presents in the most alluring terms." It does not merely say, "He *presents* His blessings." That would be a good method to use in attracting souls to Jesus. It does not even state that He presents His blessings in a *beautiful* way. That method would be even more effective. It does not declare that He presents His blessings in a *very* beautiful way. That would be better yet. But it is made very clear that Jesus presents His blessings "in the *most alluring* terms." "I will allure her." *That* is superlative language. "He is not content merely to announce these blessings."—*Ibid.*

We would surely think we were doing well if we merely announced the blessings that come to those who leave the world and follow in the Christian pathway. But God is not content with any mere announcement of these blessings. "He presents them in the *most attractive way,* to excite a desire to possess them."—*Ibid. That* is Christ's method, and I thank God for it.

Christ, who is our maker, tells us that the fundamental law of His government is love (1 John 4:8). And closely associated with love is the power of choice (Joshua 24:15).

And love cannot function without choice. It is left for each one to "*let* this mind be in you, which was also in Christ Jesus" (Phil. 2:5). Therefore, God *cannot,* and *will not, compel* anyone. The right to *choose* is the sovereign right of every human being. Like a sacred circle it surrounds the soul. Even God, almighty though He is, will not *decide* for us. We all know that. Then why should *we* try to decide for another, since even *God* will not? Jesus makes Himself and His blessings so attractive that the human soul will choose Him. There is nothing complicated about that method. It is very simple.

OUR METHOD

Now, notice again with me *our* method, which has failed, like the method of the unsuccessful poultryman. "The young are often urged to do duty, to speak or pray in meeting; urged to die to pride. Every step they are urged. Such religion is *worth nothing*."—*Testimonies,* vol. 1, p. 162. When we employ such methods, it shows that our religion, our philosophy, is not that of Christ. It is worth nothing.

If we have a religion that will not save others, we may well check to make sure whether it has saved us. "That religion which will not exert a regenerating power upon the world, is of *no value.* We cannot trust it for our own salvation. The sooner we cast it away the better; for it is powerless and spurious."—*Ibid.,* vol. 5, p. 389.

If our methods have not saved others, then they cannot save us. So we had better get a new philosophy—a new religion.

It is not an easy thing for people to cast away anything that clings like a sandbur or a sticktight. If we take it off our clothing, it clings to our hand. And if we then endeavor to remove it from our hand, it may be back on our clothing again. So is the *spurious* religion of urging, of criticism, instead of love; of denunciation instead of an alluring, winning philosophy that points to Him who is "altogether lovely." Let us cast away that spurious, or counterfeit, method.

"Could we now leave the cold, traditional sentiments which hinder our advancement, we would view the work of saving souls in an altogether different light."—*The Review and Herald,* May 6, 1890. It is this "different light" that I pray God may send us. Christ wants to give us rest from our methods that are burdensome and hard to bear. He invites us to "learn of me," for His method is easy, and His burden is light (Matt. 11:28, 29).

WHAT ABOUT WARNINGS?

Perhaps there is someone who is saying to himself, "Yes, I believe what you say is right, up to a certain point. But what about the warning portions of the Word of God?"

That is a good question too. I think it deserves a very frank answer. In fact, I believe it may prove to be a real eye opener to many of us. Let us notice briefly some of the most severe warnings of the Bible, and study them very carefully.

As I sat one Sabbath beside a fellow minister in the study just before church service, he said to me, "I wish you could have been in the class I was in today. They had a very interesting discussion." Then he told me that during the study of the day's lesson a very sincere member of the class told how she had that very week gone out and denounced people for their ways. She had condemned them by crying aloud and sparing not. Then she quoted Isaiah 58:1 as authority for her methods: "Cry aloud, spare not, lift up thy voice like a trumpet, and shew my people their transgression, and the house of Jacob their sins."

So in my sermon I pointed out that the message of Isaiah 58 is not one commanding the church members to go out and condemn and denounce their unbelieving friends and neighbors. It is rather to "cry aloud" and "shew *my* people"—not unbelievers—*"their* transgression, and the house of Jacob"—not non-Christians—*"their* sins."

This scripture is not a command to denounce *other* people, but it is a rebuke to God's professing people. And what does it especially rebuke, among other things? Why, it rebukes us for our spirit of denouncing other people. "Behold, *ye* fast for strife and *debate"* (Isa. 58:4). This is a strong message from God—not to the world, but to the church. The people who *profess* to love God, love to *debate.* They who should be reflecting the love of God are smiting "with the fist of wickedness" (Isa. 58:4). Instead of condemning and denouncing, they should be revealing the love of Jesus by undoing "the heavy burdens," loosing "the bands of wickedness," letting "the oppressed go free," and dealing their "bread to the hungry" (Isa. 58:6, 7).

God is commanding His ministers here to "cry aloud" to His own people who are covetous and ease loving. God's ministers are to "cry aloud" and "spare not," telling God's professing people to share their blessings with those less fortunate, rather than to hoard them selfishly and criticize and condemn others. God's people—according to these verses—have been denunciatory rather than kind and loving. They have had the spirit of condemnation rather than the spirit of sacrifice. They love to examine the lives of others rather than to examine their own lives.

What a sad commentary! A group of people who themselves are a covetous, debating, condemning people think that the very message that condemns them, and is given to bring them to their senses, is directed to others. Thus it does them no good. In Christ's ministry He only denounced the denouncer, the hypocrites. So let us lay down the "burden of denouncing," and learn of Jesus.

It is no wonder that Jesus pleads with His own Laodicean church. He says, "Because thou sayest, *I* am *rich,* and increased with goods, and have need of nothing; and knowest not that *thou* art wretched, and miserable, and poor, and blind, and naked:" "I will spue thee out of my mouth" (Rev. 3:17, 16).

So the "cry aloud, spare not" of Isaiah 58 is against a debating, covetous, professed Sabbathkeeping church.

"BABYLON IS FALLEN"

At a recent camp meeting where I conducted a series of studies on soul winning, I invited written questions on the topic under discussion. One man turned in the question: "What are you going to do about Revelation 14:8, 'Babylon is fallen, is fallen'?"

I replied that Revelation 14:6 gives the setting. It declares that we are to give the "everlasting gospel." And gospel is "good news." We had better be careful not to be so busy talking about "Babylon is fallen" that we fail to give the "gospel" also. We must see there a balanced message. The gospel is the only hope for those who are in fallen Babylon. Therefore, to leave the gospel out would be to defeat the whole purpose of the warning. God warns that He may save. This is why Revelation 14:6-12 makes the "gospel" even more prominent than the fact that "Babylon is fallen."

In studying the warning messages of Revelation 14:6-12, I am led to admire the wonderful tact God has used in giving them. Symbols are used so that no one can take offense. Great truths are shrouded in symbolic language, so that those who do not wish to know cannot find occasion against the message or messengers. "Without a parable

40

spake he not unto them" (Matt. 13:34). We should be as careful, as tactful, as full of wisdom, as was Jesus. But in order to be like Him, we must come to Him with our pride, our self-sufficiency, our superior attitude; and fall at His feet in deep humility, asking His pardon for our unkindness in dealing with those who may not have received as much gospel light as we have.

It is true that a messenger boy in hiring out to Western Union has no right to state that he will deliver only pleasant and positive messages. Should he state when he applies for the job, "I will only deliver messages of congratulations, weddings, birthdays, birth announcements, anniversaries, et cetera. I do not like negatives, so I will not deliver messages of bereavement, of accident, or of death." "Foolish," you say. "Of course such a one could not be hired by Western Union."

True, God's messengers, whether they be ministers or laymen, must deliver *all* God's messages. But we must give them as Jesus did if we would win souls as Jesus won them. Let us never forget that in the message to come out of Babylon, God uses the term *"my* people." Therefore, we have no right to infer that people of another faith are not God's people. The most severe warning of the Bible indicates that people of other faiths may be *"my* people." When you and I visit with people of other religious faiths, let us never, never even think, much less infer, that they are not God's people, as individuals.

"FIRE! FIRE!"

Some time ago I read of a public gathering in a large auditorium. During the program some of the men back stage detected a fire. Their first thought was that they must save the people in that auditorium. But *how* were they going to do it?

41

We will say that two men, Mr. Black and Mr. White, are discussing how to warn the people. Mr. Black says, "I will tell you what I think we should do. I believe I should stalk out on the stage, brush the master of ceremonies to one side without apology, since time is short, and shout, 'Fire! Fire! This building is on fire! Escape for your lives! And never say I didn't warn you.' I think that is what I had better do."

"No," says Mr. White, "I don't believe that would work. I have a better way. Let me show you." So Mr. White steps out on the stage, and begs pardon of the master of ceremonies for interrupting the gathering. Then he pulls out his watch and says to the people, "The laws of our city require that at certain times we have fire drills, so that we may know the procedure in case of an emergency. And this is one of those appointed times." And it would be, wouldn't it! "Listen closely as I give you the order to be followed in vacating this auditorium. The elderly ladies will go first, then the mothers with small children. Then will follow the older children and the old men. The younger men and women will follow. Each will use the fire exit nearest him. Now let us see," he continues, "if we can vacate this auditorium in about two minutes."

Mr. White's directions were followed. Everyone was saved. Had Mr. Black's method been used, pandemonium would have resulted, with the possibility of many being trampled underfoot in the wild effort to escape.

Had you been in that situation, which method would you have employed? I am sure I can hear you saying, "Why, Mr. White's method, of course!" Let us use as much wisdom and tact where *eternal* life is at stake. What do you say?

The very foundation of the law of God's government is love (Matt. 22:36-40). But love cannot operate without the power of choice. Each soul must make his own decision, based on the dictates of his own conscience. Therefore, anything that savors of criticism, denunciation, or belittling in order to bring about the decision we desire, is a form of force. It is therefore unchristian.

FOLLOW JESUS' METHOD

How then can we help a person to come to a decision for Christ? Only by using Christ's methods. "His blessings He presents in the most alluring terms. He is not merely content to announce these blessings. He presents them in the most attractive way to excite a desire to possess them." —*The Desire of Ages*, p. 826.

Only as we "excite a desire" to possess Christ can we expect souls to decide for Him. By picturing Him as the one "altogether lovely," we "excite a desire to possess" Him. By showing the advantages of the gospel, we "excite a desire to possess" it. By making truth attractive, we "excite a desire to possess" it. There is no other rule by which we have a right to represent Christ or His gospel. Controversy is out. Condemnation has no place in soul winning. Denunciation is foreign to the method by which Christ won the sinful, the wanderer, the lost, to Himself.

"ALLURE," "ENAMOR"

Christ reveals His methods when He states, "I will allure her." That sounds like the father of the prodigal. He met his wayward son while he was yet a great way off. He kissed that unkempt face. He cleaned up that filthy body, and in exchange for his rags placed on him the best robe. He put new shoes on his feet. He slew the fatted calf. He rejoiced over him with singing, and made merry.

And *that* is God. God knows how to attract the sinner. The Scriptures declare that God does more than instruct

43

—He reconciles. "When we were enemies, we were *reconciled* to God by the death of his Son" (Rom. 5:10). Wonderful alluring power of the gospel! Ours is a ministry, not of denunciation or condemnation, but of reconciliation. "God . . . hath given to us the ministry of reconciliation" (2 Cor. 5:18).

"If Christ be in us the hope of glory, we shall discover such matchless charms in Him that the soul will be enamored."—*Testimonies,* vol. 1, p. 162.

Love Awakens Love

A woman once came to Dr. George W. Crane for advice.

"Dr. Crane," she began, "I hate my husband, and I want to hurt him. Will you tell me how to do it?"

Dr. Crane replied, "Why, certainly. How do you think you would like to hurt him?"

"I think I want to divorce him," she replied, "because he has fallen in love with somebody else."

"Oh," replied Dr. Crane, "if he has fallen in love with another woman, a divorce from you is probably what he would like. That would not hurt him now. Before you divorce him, you must make him fall in love with you. Then when you divorce him it will hurt him."

"Oh, good!" she exclaimed. "Now, Doctor, tell me how to make him fall in love with me so I can hurt him."

The doctor quietly, and with a twinkle in his eye, replied, "I'll tell you how. Give him three honest compliments a day."

"Oh, I see," she responded. And then—she hesitated. "But what is there about him I could compliment?"

The doctor guided her bewildered thinking, "Does he dress well?"

"Oh, yes, he does," came the quick reply.

"Well," observed Dr. Crane, "you drop the remark in his hearing that he chooses becoming ties, or that he wears his clothes well."

Guiding her again, the doctor queried, "Is he good looking?"

"Oh," she exclaimed, "he's handsome."

"Well," continued the wise doctor, "*you* tell him so."

Looking into her puzzled face, the doctor again inquired, "Does he support the family?"

"Yes," came back the answer again, "he is a *good* provider."

"Then," continued the doctor, "tell him that, too. And as you give him the three honest compliments, others will come to you. And the man will fall in love with you. *Then* you can hurt him."

"Oh," she said, "good! Thank you, Doctor."

"Return in about six months," directed the doctor, "and I will explain the next step to take." And with that, the woman was gone.

Several months later she was back again in Dr. Crane's office. Her face was beaming. "Doctor, it works!" she exclaimed. "My husband is madly in love with me."

"Fine!" replied the doctor. "*Now* divorce him."

"But, Dr. Crane," stammered the delighted wife, "I don't want to divorce him now. I love him too."

Of course Dr. Crane knew all the while that that would be the outcome of what seemed to be a very difficult problem. And all the wife had done was to obey a simple command to let "the wife see that she reverence her husband" (Eph. 5:33).

MAKES HOMES HAPPY

I told this incident one morning in church, and then recommended, "Now, men, let us go home this morning

45

and tell our wives that we love them. We may shock them a bit," I added, "but let's do it anyway. You know before we were married we used to talk love to them. Why not go home and try it all over again?"

There was a big man sitting there that morning who had been attending the meetings the entire week. I had noticed that he appeared to be rather unhappy. That evening it was my privilege to go out to his home to bring him and his wife to church. On the way this gentleman said to me, "Brother Coon, do you remember what you recommended to us this morning?"

"Yes," I answered, smiling a bit.

"Well, I went back home and practiced it on my wife," he began. "I went up to her and exclaimed, 'I love you.' And what do you think she replied, Brother Coon?"

"What *did* she say?" I was eager to know.

"She turned incredulously toward me and snapped back, 'What's wrong with you? Are you crazy?' But I repeated my former loving proclamation, 'I really do love you.' 'What's happened?' she persisted." Then he said, "I kept on telling her that I loved her until I finally convinced her that I really did." And he turned to her there in the back seat and whispered, "Didn't I, honey?"

She chuckled, "Yes, you really did." It was thrilling to see them in love with each other all over again. This man had put into practice a very simple command of Scripture: "Husbands, love your wives, even as Christ also loved the church, and gave himself for it" (Eph. 5:25).

Friends, that is Christianity. That is the true religion of Jesus Christ in the home; Jesus in the neighborhood; Jesus everywhere we go. Without it we are no better than were the Israelites of Jesus' day "to whom pertaineth the adoption, and the glory, and the covenants, and the giving of the law, and the service of God, and the promises" (Rom.

9:4). They had everything but *Jesus*. Him they rejected. And without *Him,* all their other wonderful possessions were worth *nothing,* for they crucified Jesus.

It has been rightly observed that "a belief in the theory of the truth is not enough. To present this *theory* to unbelievers *does not* constitute you a witness for Christ." —*The Review and Herald,* Feb. 3, 1891. In all human experience a theoretical knowledge of the truth has never proved to be sufficient for the saving of the soul. But we can get people to fall in love with Jesus. There is one "altogether lovely." We can save sinners, not by presenting an abstract doctrine, but by reflecting the character of the Master. Then they may sing from their hearts:

> Earthly pleasures vainly call me;
> I would be like Jesus;
> Nothing worldly shall enthrall me;
> I would be like Jesus.

A loving Christian is one whose presence the children enjoy. He is one whom the wife or husband loves to be near. But we have not always been like Jesus. Could it be that that is the reason why we have not been able to bring more souls to the Master? May it be that we have presented *abstract* truth instead of practical love—love that woos, love that allures, love that enamors? I would exchange a thousand cold truths for one loving Jesus, wouldn't you? For *He* is "altogether lovely." But why not combine Jesus and scriptural truth? The Lord in the Lord's *day* gives it delight. The Master in stewardship brings the servant joy. Jesus must be the center, the joy, the delight of it all. And we must be lovely ourselves if we expect others to *choose* the One *we* love.

It is amazing how some Christians have the impression that the religion of Christ is not a contribution to them personally. They think it is a sacrifice. But Jesus wants us to change our conception. When Peter came to Christ saying, "We have forsaken all, and followed thee; what shall we have therefore?" (Matt. 19:27), Jesus made clear to him that they would have persecution. But He did *not* say, "You will not get much out of this life. You will have to go through life moaning and sighing. Your heads must be bowed down like a bulrush." Oh, no! Jesus did not say that.

10,000 PER CENT INTEREST

Do you know what Jesus replied? He said to Peter, "You will receive one hundredfold in this life!" That amounts to 10,000 per cent interest on our investment. You figure it out! That is 10,000 per cent interest! Why, my friends, if one of you businessmen could go down to a bank and convince the banker that by lending you a thousand dollars, the bank would get 10,000 per cent interest on its investment, the banker would fall head over heels for such a plan. Now wouldn't he?

You and I are to prove to the world that true Bible Christianity is a great contribution. It will give them 10,000 per cent interest on their investment. Thus wise men will decide to make that kind of an investment. It is only logical that they should. It is only reasonable to believe that they will.

My friends, it is our duty to present the blessings of Jesus in such an attractive, such an alluring manner, that we will "excite" in others a desire to possess them. God is pleased with even the *feet* of a man who thus presents the gospel. "Behold upon the mountains the feet of him that bringeth good tidings, that publisheth peace!" (Nahum 1:15). The angels at the birth of Jesus declared, "Behold, I bring you *good* tidings of *great* joy" (Luke 2:10).

48

"ENAMORED" OF A DOG

I used to belong to a dog-hating Coon family. For years I preached against dogs. So did some of my preacher brothers. When our little daughter, Juanita, was a child, it seemed she would pick up anything that was called "dog." I did not want her collecting old stray dogs. So I said, "Juanita, if you will leave all these stray dogs alone, someday I will get a good dog for you—if there is such a thing." I promised her that, not because I liked dogs. Oh, no! It was merely the easiest way out of what to me was a real problem.

Then one day I went to sympathize with a man who had lost his wife. As I walked into his home I saw there a little toy pomeranian. And what do you suppose that little creature did? She stood up on her hind legs, put her front paws right up to me, and told me in her doggy language that she thought a lot of me. And do you know, she *allured* me! And I fell in love with her right there.

Her master said, "Would you like to give her a home?"

"I certainly would," was my reply. And I took that little dog home with me. My wife was out shopping. The children were in school. And, believe it or not, busy as I was, I sat down on the sofa and petted that little dog and talked lovingly to her for two hours! When my wife and children came home, she barked at everybody but me! And of course that flattered me even more!

Do you know what that little pet dog did for me? She changed my whole conception of dogs. More than once I have stopped my car to say Hello to a little pomeranian as I was traveling along the highway.

Friends, if a dog can do that by love, what can we do for others by loving and alluring them with the beautiful life of Christ in us!

WIFE CHANGED RELIGIONS

One morning in church I was speaking on the subject of winning others to Christ. In my congregation was a woman with her unbelieving husband. For twenty years she had tried to make a Christian out of him. She had used the same old method for all those many long years. It never dawned on her that she ought to try a *new* method.

A few nights later he himself told me about it. He said, "You know, as we sat there in church that morning, something happened to my wife. As you were talking about that *new* religion, she turned and kissed me on the cheek. She said, 'Honey, will you forgive me? For twenty years I have been using the wrong method on you. Will you forgive me?'"

"Brother Coon," he continued, "something happened to my wife that morning." Of course I knew what it was that had happened. The Holy Spirit had come into her heart and she was changing religions.

"I *know* she is a different woman," he said, continuing his story. "Let me tell you how I know. One of the irritations of our home was the dog. I love dogs and my wife despises them. I never asked my wife to let the dog stay in the house. I made a doghouse and kept him outside." But he gave me the impression that she had both him and the dog in the doghouse. He went on. "That was one of the chief bones of contention—the dog." Well, I knew how both of them felt, for I had been on both sides of the dog fence. "You know, after my wife kissed me in church that morning," he went on to tell me, "I came home one afternoon about three o'clock from my bus route. And what do you suppose I saw? I saw my wife and my dog out in the yard, and *she* was *petting* my *dog*. Brother Coon, I just couldn't understand it. And I am sure the dog couldn't either."

So her husband *knew* she had changed religions. You see, she herself also was conscious of a changed philosophy. A wonderful letter we received from her later lamented her wasted years of using the old nagging method.

Truly, there is something about the real religion of Jesus Christ that makes us kind even to the pets. It allures the children. It creates a sweeter fellowship between husband and wife, between parents and children; among playmates, as well as in neighborhoods, communities, and nations. Friends, it *is* possible to change our method when God fulfills His promise to give us new hearts of love (Eze. 36:26; Rom. 5:5).

NEW CONVERTS USE IT

A new convert to Christ had a great burden for her husband. "May I suggest to you how you may win him?" I asked. Of course she was eager to know. "Return home and just *love* your husband. Be a sweetheart to him. If there is a certain kind of roast he likes better than any other kind, be sure he has it often. If he is especially fond of a certain kind of pie, bake it for him. If there are certain things about the keeping of the home that he especially appreciates, be sure these are not neglected. Do everything possible to please him, without compromising your allegiance to God. In other words, just do everything you can to demonstrate real love for him."

About ten days later a man came to see me. He said, "Mr. Coon, I've got the most wonderful wife in all the world since she joined your church! Tell me more about it."

Friends, if you have failed to win men and women to Christ, do not become discouraged. Christ will give you a new heart. "If any man be in Christ, he is a new creature" (2 Cor. 5:17). Will you not fall on your knees right now and ask God to make you that "new creature" in Him? Then you will "allure" people as Jesus did, for He will dwell inside. Souls will be "enamored" into deciding for Him because "I live; yet not I, but Christ liveth in me" (Gal. 2:20).

I need Jesus in my life today. I must have Him in my home. I crave Him in everything I do, don't you? When the One who is "altogether lovely" shines out of our lives, out of our studies, out of our conversation, out of our every act of life, then people will come to Him in multiplied numbers. I believe that with all my heart. They will be *allured* to Him, and *enamored* with Him. The drawing power of the gospel will be so much stronger than the lure of the world that they will of their own free will choose Jesus.

TELL THE WORLD

A great church leader stood up in a missionary convention and said, "I would not cross the street to give India a new theology. She has more theology now than she knows what to do with. I would not cross the street to give China a new code of ethics. Her present code is far higher than her present ethics. I would not cross the street to bring Japan a new religious literature. She already has a richer literature than religious life. But I would travel around the world again and again, God willing, to tell India and China and Japan, and the rest of the world, that—

> There is a fountain filled with blood,
>   Drawn from Immanuel's veins;
> And sinners plunged beneath that flood,
>   Lose all their guilty stains.

And I would too, wouldn't you? It is because "His

52

mouth is most sweet: yea, he is altogether lovely. This is my beloved, and this is my friend" (Song of Sol. 5:16).

"In Christ is the tenderness of the shepherd, the affection of the parent, and the matchless grace of the compassionate Saviour. His blessings He presents in the most alluring terms. He is not content merely to announce these blessings; He presents them in the most attractive way, to excite a desire to possess them. So His servants are to present the riches of the glory of the unspeakable Gift. The wonderful love of Christ will melt and subdue hearts, when the mere reiteration of doctrines would accomplish nothing."—*The Desire of Ages,* p. 826.

Jesus Prepares You

~~~~~~

*F*IVE YEARS ago I was a drunkard. When my wife and I were married, neither of us gave a thought to God or religion. I was at that time one of the managers of a great linen company of America." So spoke a stranger standing beside me.

I had taken my car to a Gulf station just a few miles from one of our large Southern cities, and had it there on the grease rack. This stranger and I had met in rather a singular fashion. When he came in where I was standing I thought perhaps he was the manager of the filling station. He greeted me with, "How are you?"

"I am happy," I responded. And he looked at me as though he could not quite understand why anyone should be so happy. I let him know that it was my love for Jesus that made me happy.

Then he looked me full in the face and said, "I take Him with me everywhere I go."

"Oh," I exclaimed, "tell me more about it!"

DISCHARGED!

"I was a drunkard without God and without hope. I gradually grew worse. My company was very kind to me, hoping that I would be cured of the liquor habit. They transferred me from place to place, hoping to salvage me. But all to no avail.

"They finally had to notify me that they could no longer use me as manager. That was the most terrible blow of my life," he added. "If a relative had died, I am sure I could not have felt it more keenly. However, they did tell me I could work for them as an ordinary salesman. Humiliating though that was, since there was nothing else for me to do, I began all over again as a green salesman! The blow was terrific!

"Then I began to come to myself. My wife and I talked it over. We came to the conclusion that what we needed was God. So we decided to go to church the next Sunday. We attended about three weeks, and then we both accepted Christ as our Saviour. We joined the Baptist Church. I did not get drunk any more, but I still drank cocktails and liquor occasionally. I also smoked and attended the movies and dances. With this slight change of conduct, I continued attending church for three years.

NEW RESOLUTION!

"And then one morning in church I made a new resolution. The preacher was telling the story of the paralytic who was brought to Jesus. He said, 'You know they brought him on a cot. It "was borne of four." So there must have been a man at each corner. None of them could have healed the man. Probably none of them could even teach, or sing, or preach. But each could carry the corner of the cot and take the poor sufferer to Jesus.'

"As the preacher was speaking that morning, I said, 'Lord, that's just me. I can't preach. I can't pray. I can't sing. I can't talk publicly for You. But, Lord Jesus, I am willing to take the corner of a cot and bring somebody to

Sunday school and church. Maybe that way I will bring them to Jesus.'

"At the close of the sermon I walked up to the preacher and said, 'I'll make an agreement with you. But I want you to understand now what it is. I am willing to take the corner of a cot and bring people to Sunday school and church. But it is with this explicit understanding: if you ever ask me to pray publicly, or talk, or preach, or sing—any one of those four things—our agreement is canceled. And I'll never have another thing to do with this church.'

"The preacher replied, 'I agree to that. I will never ask you to do any one of those four things you have mentioned.'

"'All right,' I agreed, 'then I'll go out and take the corner of a cot.'

"I decided to go to the hardware store and buy a big ball. I would give that ball to a young man in the church and say to him, 'Now anybody you can find who will come to Sunday school next week, but who has no transportation, write his name on this ball. Then you give the ball to me and I will pick him up and take him to church in my car.'

"As I was explaining this plan to the salesman at the hardware store, he volunteered to give me another ball. I gave the balls to two young men.

"The first Sunday I had two people to take to church. But before long I had so many passengers I had to make two trips. My friend, who had a Packard, was doing the same. The interest increased, and the group kept growing until our church bought a bus. And we filled that bus. By this time we had a route established. I was going out on that bus route, inviting everyone who did not attend any church, to come to our church. And I found myself relating to them a bit of my own experience in finding Jesus.

"After a few weeks we bought another bus, and started another route. Each bus carried more than fifty persons to Sunday school and church. Then we purchased the third bus, and sent it out on still another route. Then the fourth bus was purchased. And then the fifth, the sixth, the seventh, an eighth bus, then a ninth. Now we have ten buses operating every Sunday.

"I purchased a sound projector, films, and a screen to use as I bore my testimony to my wonderful Jesus. I thought, 'That machine can talk when I can't.' And then, almost before I realized it, I was giving my experience in Christ—really preaching!

"It began in a remarkable way when I was invited to visit the jail. Some Christian friends asked me to give my personal experience to the inmates. This I did with an ease that surprised me. That was the real beginning of my preaching experience. I would put up my screen in any available place, one of which was a tourist court where I did business as a salesman for the linen company I represent. I have had as many as 175 persons at a single service. I was preaching before or after the picture. They were sort of revival sermons. The Lord richly blessed me. And now I hold revivals every opportunity my work will permit.

"It all began two years ago. That morning when I decided to take the corner of a cot, I said to the Lord, 'Lord, I can't invite people to Jesus if I still go to the movies, and keep on smoking, dancing, drinking cocktails, and so on. I am laying them all at the foot of the cross. And from that day to this I have never indulged in any of those questionable pleasures.

"Oh," he said reverently, "I take Him with me everywhere I go."

57

"About how many are you bringing each week to Sunday school and church?" I queried.

"About five hundred and fifty. It is quite an organization now," he explained.

"Could you tell me about how many you have won to Jesus during these two years since you fully surrendered to the Lord?" I again questioned.

He hesitated a moment. His countenance was full of the love of God. Then he answered very quietly and humbly, "About two thousand."

I was especially interested in this Christian gentleman's work for souls because he himself had made a complete surrender. Otherwise, two thousand souls might not mean very much. But when a man parts company with every cherished idol, then we may know that his experience is deep. It has a real foundation. He can then show sinners the way to God.

How He Did It

Let us analyze for a moment the steps this dear man took in the great change from drunkard to revivalist.

First—he came to the place where he distrusted himself. He recognized that he was a failure. He had been dismissed from his position of responsibility.

Second—then he came to God.

Third—he united his surrendered weakness to God's strength, his ignorance to God's wisdom, his unworthiness to Christ's merits, and went out to do the little that he could. The Lord increased his talent exceedingly. These three steps are simple. But they are within the reach of every person who is willing to take them.

Someone has worded the first step in soul winning as "self-distrust." "The first thing to be learned by all who would become workers together with God is the lesson of self-distrust."—*The Desire of Ages,* p. 250. Jesus set us an example, when in His humanity He declared, "I can of mine own self do nothing" (John 5:30). Every person who has ever been a successful soul winner has taken this step. He recognizes that he is of himself a failure. If he is to succeed, he must unite with divine power.

Let us look at the experience of Peter. When he caught a vision of Christ, he cried out in self-distrust, "I am a sinful man, O Lord" (Luke 5:8). Then Jesus assigned him a soul-winning task. "From henceforth thou shalt catch men," was the promise of the Master (Luke 5:10). Simple formula? Yes, but effective.

Then there is Isaiah. Describing one of his visions, he exclaimed, "I saw . . . the Lord" (Isa. 6:1). The glorious revelation wrung from his lips the cry, "Woe is me! for I am undone; because I am a man of unclean lips, . . . for mine eyes have seen the King." As if in answer to his confession an angel came and touched his lips with a live coal from off the altar. Then he heard the voice of the Lord saying, "Whom shall I send, and who will go for us?" And Isaiah, trembling with the sense of his unworthiness, but delighted with the prospect of partnership with God, cried out, "Here am I; send me." And the Lord replied, "Go."

Now we see Jeremiah, that child prophet. The story is recorded in Jeremiah the first chapter. He caught a picture of the Lord. Then he said, "I cannot speak: for I am a child." He distrusted himself. "Then the Lord put forth his hand, and touched my mouth. And the Lord said unto me, Behold, I have put my words in thy mouth." It was Jeremiah who was the great prophet of God during the early part of the Babylonian captivity.

Next is Daniel. Sensing the presence of the Holy One, he exclaimed, "My comeliness was turned in me into

59

corruption" (Dan. 10:8). He abhorred himself. Then the angel said, "O Daniel, a man greatly beloved, understand the words that I speak unto thee." Daniel was used of God to pen a vision of that beautiful time prophecy that points out the very year of Christ's baptism, His death, and the rejection of the Jewish nation, together with the date of the beginning of the great investigative judgment that is taking place in heaven today. What a precious, priceless heritage for the church to the very close of time!

How did it come about? By humility. He realized he was nothing. Then he was strengthened by the Lord. And in uniting his weakness with God's strength, Daniel became mighty. By connecting his ignorance with the Lord's wisdom, he became one of the wisest men of his generation. And by uniting his unworthiness to Christ's holiness, he became "greatly beloved" by heaven itself. We too can have that experience. It is not beyond us or above us. It is not too deep a mystery. The law of soul winning is very simple. We must distrust *self*. And then God gives strength, wisdom, courage, and holiness.

John the Baptist declared that he was not worthy even to unloose the shoes of the Master. He rose to the tremendous height of self-abnegation! No wonder Christ declared that of all the prophets ever born, none was greater than John the Baptist. We too may share his experience. This is not accomplished by endeavoring to appear learned, or deep, or impressive. It does not come by self-seeking, self-supremacy, or self-sufficiency. Such an experience comes *only* by placing *self* at the foot of the cross.

Now notice Paul, the chief of New Testament missionaries. It was he who said that of *sinners* "I am chief." And what caused him to view himself in such a light? He had caught a vision of the crucified Christ. He was used of

God to pen fourteen books of the New Testament. This was accomplished through a man who did not trust himself, his own learning, his own righteousness. He had learned the lesson that "I can of mine own self do nothing."

THE REASON FOR OUR FAILURE

Why is it that we are not winning more souls to Christ? We do well to consider. May it not be that we have not fully surrendered *self* to Christ. I do not refer to "surrender" in the sense of accepting Jesus as our Saviour, merely, but in the actual experience of *dying to self*. "This is why, in choosing the instruments for his work, the Lord passes by those whom the world honors as great, talented, and brilliant. They are too often proud and self-sufficient. They feel competent to act without counsel from God."—*Patriarchs and Prophets*, p. 554.

But the drunkard who became a revivalist knew he was a failure. He distrusted himself. He knew he could not do anything without superhuman help. All friends had proved insufficient. Now he gave up *self* to God. We Christians who are drunk with *self* must also fall at the foot of the cross. Let us confess that we become offended easily if someone does not recognize our talents or efforts as we think he should. Like Isaiah, we must cry out, "Woe is me!" And like poor Peter, "I am a sinful man, O Lord."

"Those who have had the deepest experience in the things of God, are the farthest removed from pride or self-exaltation. They have the humblest thoughts of self, and the most exalted conceptions of the glory and excellence of Christ."—*Testimonies*, vol. 5, p. 223. But the glorious privilege of winning souls is denied all who refuse to die to self. "Their service is marred by desire for supremacy. . . . Here is one of the chief secrets of failure in Christian work."—*Christ's Object Lessons*, p. 47.

"There is nothing so offensive to God or so dangerous to the human soul as *pride* and *self-sufficiency*. Of all sins it is the most *hopeless*, the most *incurable*."—*Ibid.*, p. 156. All this must be laid aside. Then "the most childlike disciple is the most efficient in labor for God."—*The Desire of Ages*, p. 436.

WILLIE

Willie Brinninger had an impediment in his speech. He stammered and stuttered. It was almost impossible to make out anything he was saying.

But Willie wanted to work for Jesus. He longed to win souls. He saw in one of the church papers an invitation to attend a colporteurs' convention, where he could learn to sell Christian literature. The offer was open to all who would come and learn their canvass. They would receive board and accommodations during the convention, without charge. They also were to be given their transportation. More than that, the promise was that if they attended the classes faithfully and learned the canvass well, they would be authorized to sell the literature and be given territory to work.

Pastor Dickerson taught the class. But when the class was over, some of the leaders were about to reject Willie. They said, "He will bring reproach on the work of God." "It will be an insult to send Willie out to the homes of the people to sell Christian books, with such a glaring impediment in his speech," they thought.

But Pastor Dickerson replied, "We have given him our word. We even published it in the official paper. We must keep our word. He has fulfilled his part. He has memorized his canvass perfectly, as well as we can ascertain." And so they decided to let Willie go out and try to sell books.

In a short period of time Willie was sending in big

reports to the office. The superintendent and others were sure Willie had made a mistake. "Why," they said, "evidently Willie does not even know how to make out his report."

So one of the officers went down to see what was wrong with Willie. They must take action at once if Willie was falsifying his work.

"You take the first house this morning," said Willie's superior as they started out, "and I will take the next. But we will go together. I am eager to see how you sell so many books." Willie agreed.

As they neared the first house out on the country road Willie motioned to his companion. He followed Willie to a tree just beside the road. There Willie fell on his knees. He mumbled his stammering prayer to God. Tears were trickling down his cheeks. Then they rose, went to the first house, and knocked on the door. The knock was heard by the woman inside. She came to the door, and Willie gave the canvass for his book.

As Willie gave his exhibition he turned the book so the woman could see the pictures and read snatches here and there. No one knew what Willie was saying. But he went through his entire canvass. Then he pointed out the prices of the various bindings and showed them to the woman. He also pointed to the dates of delivery printed there. As he pulled out his order pad he showed her where she should place her signature. The customer placed her name on the dotted line.

Willie's partner canvassed the next house. Then it was Willie's turn. Again he beckoned for his companion to follow him to the side of the country road and under another tree. There once more they knelt in prayer. Willie again implored Heaven for help and for the Holy Spirit to impress the heart of his customer, although his words could not be understood. They rose and made their way to the door of the next farmhouse. He gave his exhibition, and again received an order for his good book. And that is why Willie was turning in such large sales reports to the office.

About a year later, at a camp meeting, Pastor Dickerson's son, age fourteen, met a young man who was preparing for baptism. Young Dickerson inquired of the boy, "What caused you to become interested in the church?"

"I bought a book from Willie Brinninger," was his reply.

"But why did you purchase the book from Willie?" was his eager question.

"I felt that I *must* have that book," was his earnest answer. And now he was to be baptized into the Lord Jesus Christ.

Willie determined to overcome his impediment. Young Dickerson spied him one day sitting all alone under a tree, with a book in his hand, struggling to pronounce the words without stammering. His persistence was great. It intrigued the youthful Dickerson. Willie was blessed of the Lord, and overcame his stammering. Later, for a time, he topped the sales record for all the colporteurs in North America.

How Willie Did It

How do such men—such inadequate men—succeed? I am sure you have already discovered the answer. "The Lord can work most effectually through those who are most sensible of their own insufficiency, and who will rely upon Him as their leader and source of strength. He will make them strong by uniting their weakness to His might, and wise by connecting their ignorance with His wisdom."—*Patriarchs and Prophets,* p. 553.

Where We Fail

We often try to unite our *strength* to God's strength. But Heaven accepts no such offer. It must be a union of our *weakness* with His *strength*. It *cannot* be a mixture of our *wisdom*, but of our *ignorance*, with His wisdom. The eleventh chapter of Hebrews speaks of many of the great men of faith, and tells us how they became giants for God. This explanation is hidden away in a lone verse of Scripture. Here it is, "Out of weakness [they] were made strong" (Heb. 11:34). It does not say that out of *strength* they were made strong. But like the drunkard, and Willie; like Isaiah and Peter; like John the Baptist and Saint Paul, they distrusted self. They recognized that they were weak, unworthy, insufficient. Then out of that very element of weakness, united with God's strength, *they* were made strong. Wonderful, wonderful secret!

Why has God chosen this method? "That no flesh should glory in his presence." "God hath chosen the foolish things of the world to confound the wise; and God hath chosen the weak things of the world to confound the things which are mighty; and base things of the world, and things which are despised, hath God chosen, yea, and things which are not, to bring to nought things that are: that no flesh should glory in his presence" (1 Cor. 1:27-29).

Wonderful Secret

Here, then, is the wonderful secret of successful service for the Master. *Self* becomes a nail upon the wall, holding the picture of Jesus in its place. It is eager to show only the wonder, the grace, the beauty, and the salvation of Jesus Christ. *Self* is completely hidden behind the beautiful Jesus. "Those who have had the deepest experience in the things of God . . . feel that the lowest place in His

5   65

service is too honorable for them."—*Testimonies,* vol. 5, p. 223. And why? Because they have learned the lesson the drunkard learned. They come to the place in their experience that Willie did. They have followed the pattern of the Bible giants of faith. They feel their insufficiency. The self-confident do not feel their need. But when a person comes to the place where he recognizes that he can of himself do nothing, and reaches up by faith and takes hold of the hand of the Infinite, then the resources of the universe are at his command!

SALT OF THE EARTH

Jesus said of His followers, "Ye are the salt of the earth" (Matt. 5:13). Of what does salt consist? It is a combination of two poisonous elements—sodium and chlorine. These two elements represent many a professed Christian. Sodium is a waxlike, unstable metal. I have seen a little chunk of sodium bubbling furiously on top of a liquid. And that, to me, represents many so-called Christians. They are so ill-tempered! *Self* asserts itself if not given recognition. It bubbles furiously. There it was. I saw it—sodium, boiling vehemently. It was all upset.

Then I have sat in the same chemistry class and heard the teacher discuss deadly chlorine. Chlorine "is a greenish, highly poisonous, liquefiable gas, with an offensive suffocating odor."—Webster's Universal Dictionary. The teacher went on to say that a little poisonous chlorine gas could empty a whole village of its inhabitants if the tank, while passing through the village, should spring a leak. Poisonous chlorine!

But you take these two dangerous elements, sodium and chlorine, put them together, and you get sodium chloride, "the salt of the earth." "Out of weakness they were made strong." This is God's formula.

66

TESTIMONY OF NATURE

Let us for a moment take a look at nature. See what a selfless thing in the natural world can accomplish by uniting with the power of God. Take, if you will, a helpless stalk of corn. Corn is only a grass. But science tells us that one stalk of corn may lift more than four hundred pounds of water in one season. Amazing, isn't it? We are also told that whereas man's suction pump can lift water only thirty-three feet at sea level, the sequoias—those giant trees of the California forest—can lift water more than three hundred feet with the greatest of ease and efficiency. What mighty power God uses day by day in nature to prove to us His willingness, His wisdom, and His power when interpreted in spiritual matters.

Friends, why do we not bring to God our weakness, that He may lift us out of ignorance into wisdom, out of sinfulness into righteousness, and out of inability into efficiency in winning souls to Christ?

JESUS ONLY CAN

The book of nature reveals nature's God—and ours. In the beginning the world was without form and void. Then God said, "Let there be light: and there *was* light" (Gen 1:3). We must come to the place where *we* are nothing. We realize that our best efforts are powerless, and have left a void within. Our lives are without form, without shape. We are frustrated and confused. Then we come to God. He brings order into our surrendered lives. Oh, there is tremendous *lifting* power in Jesus!

But we say, "How can I surrender *self?*" Listen to this: "No man can empty himself of self."—*Christ's Object Lessons,* p. 159. Isn't that amazing! I may say, "I want to empty myself of self so that I can be a partner with God." And yet no man can do it. "No man can empty himself of self." But this is what we *can* do—"we can only consent for Christ to accomplish the work. Then the language of the soul will be, 'Save me in spite of myself, my weak, un-Christlike self. Lord, take my heart; for I cannot give it. It is Thy property. Keep it pure, for I cannot keep it for Thee. Mold me, fashion me, raise me into a pure and holy atmosphere, where the rich current of Thy love can flow through my soul.' "—*Ibid.*

How

Again I hear someone say, "I have looked to Jesus. I have renounced self. Now I start working for souls. But does self have to be renounced any more after I start?"

How about that? Do you recall how Paul wrote, "I die *daily*" (1 Cor. 15:31)? "It is not only at the beginning of the Christian life that this renunciation of self is to be made. At every advance step heavenward it is to be renewed."—*Ibid.*, pp. 159, 160. How often am I to renounce self? Every day; and every time through the day when self tries to assert itself.

The husband comes home and finds the wife has burned the beans. He does not like to eat burned beans. Now, that is a good time to renounce self. Instead of making some unkind remark to her—which self would feel like doing—instead of that, he says, "That's perfectly all right, honey. Accidents happen to the best of people." Thus he renounces self. *Self* longs to come to the front. *Self* craves recognition. But *self* must be renounced.

The little girl accidentally knocks a precious heirloom from the mantel. It breaks in a dozen pieces. Mother knows it was purely an accident. It was something she herself might have done. But the prized treasure was smashed.

That is a good time for mother to renounce self. That is a *good* time to do it. You know, it is an easy thing for us all to renounce self when everything is going smoothly. But when we brush shoulders with the problems of life, that is a good time to renounce self. "All our good works are dependent on a power outside of ourselves."—*Ibid.,* p. 160.

That power is Christ. So we look to Jesus. We fill our souls with Him. We renounce self. Day by day we continue the process. Our minds are stayed upon Him. We continue to deplore self. Our repentance constantly deepens. Jesus daily becomes more real.

Now, having renounced self, what about the winning of souls? It is then, and then only, that the promise is ours, "I can do all things through Christ which strengtheneth me" (Phil. 4:13).

THE SPECIALIST

A church on a West Indian island felt that the people around them were hard, cold, and prejudiced. So they sent a message to headquarters requesting an evangelist. But it contained the caution, "Don't send us any ordinary evangelist. He must be a specialist. For no ordinary preacher can ever reach these prejudiced people." Did you ever feel that way? Often I hear folks talk that way about their friends and neighbors. They think they are most prejudiced and very hard.

In that church was an illiterate man. While at headquarters a search was being made for the "specialist," this illiterate man went to the elder of the church with the request: "Here's my Bible. Would you kindly underscore all the great doctrines of the Bible, each one in a different color?" We will say he was to underscore all the texts on the second coming of Christ in red; everything on the nature of man and the state of the dead in green, and so on. Well, that was a two weeks' job for the elder. And he wanted to put the poor ignorant man off. But the man kept insisting, until finally the elder acceded to his wishes and marked his Bible for him in the manner he requested.

In the meantime this illiterate man had learned from someone the titles and numbers of many songs in one of the evangelistic songbooks. Finally, with his marked Bible in his hand, and a stack of songbooks under his arm, he made his way to the city. He stationed himself on a street corner, and began to sing.

As he sang, somehow the loveliness of Jesus must have shown out through his countenance and voice, for a goodly number of people gathered around him. He passed out the songbooks. "We are singing No. 1, 'More About Jesus,' " he said smilingly. He had his songbook open. But the people did not know that he could not read a word. And they joined in the singing.

After they had enjoyed a good song service he turned to a gentleman standing beside him, a stranger, and said, "Take this Bible and read everything underscored in red, beginning with Genesis." The man read a text, and then this illiterate man, though he could not read or write, explained the text. The friend read the next text marked in the same color. And the illiterate man explained it also. And thus they continued until they had finished the lesson for the night. Then he announced when he would return. In this manner he completed a series of meetings.

While the church was looking, longing, and waiting for the "specialist," this illiterate man had *doubled* the membership of the church. He learned the lesson that all must learn—that of himself he could not win souls to the Master. So he looked to God for help, through Jesus; while others who were wiser, better educated, and probably more dignified did practically nothing.

Formula of Success

Thank God for the formula of success. First, we renounce self as we look to Jesus. Second, we let God have His way in our surrendered lives. Third, He does the work by uniting our weakness to His strength, our ignorance to His wisdom. If we ever feel strong, our usefulness is at an end. If we come to the place where we think we are wise, our service is marred. If we become self-righteous, we are immediately out of partnership with God. Only "out of weakness" does God choose to do anything to make human beings strong. And why? "That no flesh should glory in his presence" (1 Cor. 1:29).

The Prince

One night a few London policemen noticed that the door of a jewelry store was partly open. Upon investigation they detected three burglars trying to crack open the safe. In the battle that followed, the police captured one culprit, but the other two escaped. One of the officers stepped into the darkness and cried loudly for help.

A gentleman who happened along at the time saw the two robbers escaping in the night, and took both of them on. After a hand-to-hand battle he captured one, much to the delight of the officers, who asked him to accompany them to the police station as a witness against these men.

At the police station, when the gentleman was asked to give his name, he answered, "The Prince of Wales."

Friend, if *self* goes out after the jewels of self-seeking in the darkness of self-love, call loudly in your distress, and the Prince, the King of heaven, will hasten to your side. You may unite your weakness to His strength, your ignorance to His wisdom, your sinfulness to His righteousness. And then, with the Light of life, go forth and tell the world of your wonderful, wonderful Jesus!

Jesus — The Argument

~~~~~~

AN INFIDEL attended some meetings I was holding in a large tabernacle. Prior to the preaching service I always devoted about seven minutes to answering questions. Everyone enjoyed this part of the program.

But one evening, just as I was ready to leave the prayer room to go onto the rostrum, an usher handed me a set of typewritten questions someone had turned in. They were written by this infidel. There were four pages, containing twenty-eight *series* of questions. I could see at a glance they had been written by an agnostic or infidel. And the questioner added, "Please read my questions aloud to the audience, and then answer them." Of course at once I knew he wanted an argument. He wanted me to preach *his* sermon.

Do you know what my first thought was? I am ashamed to tell you, but it was: "I can nail that man to the wall with my arguments. Then I will watch him wince. He will be sorry he put in those smart questions. Yes, I will nail him with arguments. I have them. And I will use them too."

And just then I heard a voice speaking to my heart. It said, "Why not act more like Jesus than like Coon?" With that thought in mind, I began the service. As I answered a number of other questions that evening, I was all the while listening to that voice—"Why not act more like Jesus?" It seemed to be a very definite message from God to my heart.

I had answered a number of the short questions before I turned to the list written by this infidel. By that time our seven-minute question-and-answer period was about finished. We had only a moment left. But by that time the Spirit of Jesus had really pervaded my heart. As I considered his questions, I said some things that only the Lord could have helped me to say.

I began, "Friends, I have here four pages of wonderful questions. They are most intelligently written. They come from a sincere heart, I am sure. A person who would take the time to write out these questions so carefully deserves more than a moment or two of our time. I feel that the gentleman who has sent in the queries deserves to be given an hour, or perhaps longer, in their consideration. I would not wish to belittle him by attempting to answer these important questions in the few moments we have left. I think we ought to give detailed study to these splendidly written questions." With that, I laid the questions aside and preached the sermon of the evening.

A few nights later I received another letter from the same man. He said, "The way you answered my questions the other night broke my heart. I was born into a Christian home. As a boy I knelt at my mother's knee. I loved the Bible. Then as I grew up I wandered away from Christ and the teachings of His Word. I read infidel authors. Finally I turned my back on the Bible. I came to the conclusion that Christianity was a farce, and that Christians were hypocrites.

"I came to your tabernacle that night with but one

thought in mind, and that was to stir up a little strife. But when you answered my questions as you did, it broke my heart. I went home. I knelt down by my bedside. It was the first time I had knelt since I was a boy. And I gave my heart to Jesus. I told the Lord that now I knew Jesus Christ was real, for I had seen the Spirit of Jesus manifested by one of His children. Now I knew there was something to Christianity, for I had met a Christian."

Friends, as I read that letter, I could almost feel the goose pimples coming out on my arms. I thought of how nearly I had come to putting up an argument instead of revealing Jesus. I had used no argument that night. Yet I had presented the greatest argument in the world—Jesus in the life; Jesus in the words I spoke; Jesus in the tone of my voice.

JESUS DRAMATIZED HIS FATHER

Jesus, the greatest soul winner of all time, is our example. He showed us how to do right by revealing truth in His own life. He was a dramatization of His Father. "He that hath seen me," He said, "hath seen the Father" (John 14:9).

The best way to teach is through the eye. Jesus employed this method. Theory was not enough. Example was of the greatest importance to Him. He came to reveal the Father. Mere platitudes could not do it. It took a life. So "Jesus began both to *do* and teach" (Acts 1:1).

In John, chapters 6 to 8, we find a running narrative of this thought in the discussion Jesus had with the Jews. Again in the fourteenth chapter of John's Gospel we find references to the same thought. It is absolutely astonishing how Jesus presented Himself as the "way, the truth, and the life" (John 14:6).

Jesus had been telling the disciples how He was going

74

back to heaven to prepare a place for them. Then He said, "And whither I go ye know, and the way ye know" (John 14:4).

Then Thomas spoke up and retorted, "Lord, we know not whither thou goest; and how can we know the way?" (John 14:5).

Jesus gave Thomas no lengthy explanation or argument, but simply replied, "I am the way, the truth, and the life" (John 14:6). That is a wonderful statement, even *out* of context. But *in* the context it becomes one of the most *astonishing* statements of the whole Scripture. Here is a man inquiring about a physical heaven, and a physical way to get there. Jesus had been discussing that very thing with His disciples. Then He immediately throws him entirely off the track, as we would say, by apparently changing the discussion. But wait a moment! Jesus did not change the subject. He merely made crystal clear that the *way* to heaven is *Himself.* "I am the way," He began. It is not cold theory, nor abstract doctrine. Jesus says, "*I am the way.*" So we dare to reaffirm the statement that the life of Jesus was a dramatization of His Father. His life was the most wonderful moving picture this world has ever beheld! "He that hath seen me hath seen the Father" (John 14:9).

OURS TO BE LIKE HIS

We also are to be living dramas of the character of Christ. It is God's way of lighting the world. "In him was life; and the *life* was the light of men" (John 1:4).

"For even hereunto were ye called: because Christ also suffered for us, leaving us an example, that ye should follow his steps: who did no sin, neither was guile found in his mouth: who, when he was reviled, reviled not again; when he suffered, he threatened not; but committed himself to him that judgeth righteously" (1 Peter 2:21-23).

Many years ago, when I was still a boy at home, one of my elder sisters-in-law was arguing with father about how the wife should treat her husband. Father pointed out that "the Bible says the wife should 'reverence her husband.'"

"No, sir, the Bible doesn't say any such thing," returned my sister-in-law.

Whereupon my father picked up the Bible, and with a little curl of a smile on his lips, read Ephesians 5:33, "Let . . . the wife see that she reverence her husband."

"Well, *reverence* doesn't mean what I thought it did," exclaimed my sister-in-law.

Oftentimes children come to me and ask how they can honor their fathers and mothers according to the commandment (Ex. 20:12), when the parents themselves are not living good lives. Why should the wife reverence her husband when he is not worthy of it? While we think of this for a moment, here is still another command of the Lord: "Honour *all* men" (1 Peter 2:17).

"Do You mean, Lord, I should honor the drunkard?"

The answer is, "Honour *all* men."

"Do You command me, Lord, to honor the dishonest man?"

He replies, "Honour *all* men."

"Yet all men do not deserve my honor," I reply. "Why am I then commanded to 'honour all men'?"

The answer is, I am to represent the character of Christ. He honored the polluted human race to such an extent that He gave up His home in glory and died a horrible death. He loved us. He respected us—not because we were worthy, but because of what He is, and what we may be-

76

come in Him. So as we "honour all men" we are merely showing to the world what Jesus is like! We are dramatizing our Lord.

DEFERENCE

"In the advocacy of truth the *bitterest* opponents should be treated with respect and deference."—*Gospel Workers,* p. 373. "Deference" means "a yielding of opinion; submission of judgment to the opinion or judgment of another."—Webster's Universal Dictionary. And "respect" is "the act of holding in high estimation or honor."—*Ibid.* Combining these two graces, we border almost on "reverence."

We are to carry this attitude with us everywhere we go. It is a "respect," a "deference," for others. Not that they necessarily deserve it, but because we are representing Jesus. God declares that is the way to save men. "In meekness instructing those that oppose themselves; if God peradventure will give them repentance to the acknowledging of the truth" (2 Tim. 2:25). The Christlike character is the argument. It is not words merely. It is not the forcing of our own opinion upon others, but giving attention, respect, deference, to the most bitter and unworthy. By love, respect, and deference we reveal our Lord's meekness in our lives. He says, "I am meek and lowly in heart" (Matt. 11:29).

HOW IT WORKS

I am going to try to show the meaning of the word "deference."

Suppose I knock at the door of a man living some little distance from my church. "Come in," he replies, rather rough and careless.

"Good evening. My name is Coon. I am from the little red church, and I came over to invite you to——" And he does not even permit me to finish my sentence.

"Christian! Why, I've got a neighbor who's one of those things. He's no good. He goes to church every week. But he called the police when my children played on his front lawn. I don't want anything to do with a religion like that. No, don't bother me!"

"Friend, we are sorry that we have not been kind to you," I reply. "Will you forgive us?" I add, bowing graciously, and with a smile.

"W-e-l-l, I g-u-e-s-s so," the opponent replies, smiling a bit, and quite taken aback.

You know, it is amazing what a little "deference" and "respect" will do to a bitter opponent, isn't it? It's amazing! The opponent becomes my friend in a moment, when I humble myself. The words "deference" and "respect" indicate an attitude that borders almost on "reverence." Think of it! We are to be so courteous to the bitterest opponents that we almost express a "reverence" for them!

When assailed by a bitter opponent, as this gentleman, we might be tempted to bristle up and say, "You're headed for destruction. Better keep your kids at home, and not let them trample on my flower garden any more." But oh, no! "The bitterest opponents should be treated with respect and deference." This is dramatizing the spirit of Jesus.

"Remember that you are to represent Christ in His meekness and gentleness and love."—*Gospel Workers*, p. 372. "For I have given you an example," He says, "that ye should do as I have done to you" (John 13:15). "Let the prayer constantly ascend, 'Lord, teach me how to do as Jesus would do, were He in my place.'"—*Ibid.*, p. 373.

BEGINNING OF A GREAT REVIVAL

A friend of mine had an experience that made a great impression upon me. He was at the time president of a college. He had never done evangelistic work. But through a transfer of workers, he was asked to take up this line in another section of the field. He and his good wife were greatly perplexed. He felt that he did not know how to preach. His life had been devoted to teaching. Although he was now advancing in years, he followed the counsel given him and entered the pastor-evangelistic field.

The first church of which he was pastor was a little low spiritually. The members were not working together very harmoniously. But my friend immediately saw that he could not expect God to bless him in winning souls unless his own flock was at peace with one another. So he began an effort to bring about harmony in his church.

Among the objects of his labors were two women. They flatly refused to speak to each other, and had taken that attitude for some time. He knew that something must be done about this. So he got the two women together in a small room in the church. He talked to them awhile, and suggested that they shake hands and make up.

"*Me* shake hands with *her!*" one of them exclaimed. "Nothing doing! You don't know *her!*"

And then the other piped up with something like, "That woman! I will never shake *her* hand."

He prayed earnestly for guidance, and tried again to effect a reconciliation. But with the same result.

Finally he fell on his knees in prayer with the two women. As he earnestly prayed for the Holy Spirit to do the work, the miracle happened. The two women threw their arms around each other and were reconciled. The hard hearts were broken. There were tears and confessions. And a new spirit filled their hearts. And then what do you suppose happened? It was wonderful! This brother, with practically no evangelistic experience, went out and was the very first, I believe, to baptize two hundred in a single year in that difficult field.

79

Jesus touched the real key when He said, "By this shall all men know that ye are my disciples, if ye have love one to another" (John 13:35). We are to dramatize His life. We represent Him. "We are ambassadors for Christ" (2 Cor. 5:20).

"Men may combat and defy our logic, they may resist our appeals; but a life of disinterested love is an argument they cannot gainsay. A consistent life, characterized by the meekness of Christ, is a power in the world."—*The Desire of Ages,* p. 142. "I in them, and thou in me, that they may be made perfect in one; and that the world may know that thou hast sent me, and hast loved them, as thou hast loved me" (John 17:23). Think of this: The best way to prove the divinity of Christ is through the perfect unity of the church!

"The secret of our success in the work of God will be found in the harmonious working of our people. There must be concentrated action. Every member of the body of Christ must act his part in the cause of God, according to the ability that God has given him. We must press together against obstructions and difficulties, shoulder to shoulder, heart to heart."—*The Review and Herald,* Dec. 2, 1890.

The Lord invites, "Let us reason together" (Isa. 1:18). We should be logical. We should use the best arguments at our command. We should be ready to give every reason for our hope. But "the strongest argument in favor of the gospel is a loving and lovable Christian."—*The Ministry of Healing,* p. 470. "A kind, courteous Christian is the most powerful argument that can be produced in favor of Christianity."—*Gospel Workers,* p. 122.

HOLY SPIRIT'S WORK

A pastor and I were visiting some candidates for baptism. We were about ready to leave one home when the woman said, "By the way, may I ask you a question? Is it a sin for a Christian to wear a little rouge?" Her friends told her she looked sickly, and when she put on a little rouge she looked more healthy.

This prompted her question.

There was a day when I could have answered her immediately, I am afraid. But *now* when she asked the question, I claimed in my heart the promise, "If any of you lack wisdom, let him ask of God" (James 1:5-8). I cannot tell what the human heart needs. Only Christ can do that. He only can diagnose the human heart. He must put His words in my mouth. So I asked Him for wisdom. And He gave me words. "Sister," I began, "it is like this. Christianity is a growth in grace. Some have grown more into Christ than others. I do not know how far you have grown."

And as she looked wonderingly and smiled, the pastor added, "I'll tell you, sister, what to do. You talk it over with the Lord. And whatever *He* tells you to do will be all right with us."

She replied, "That's the trouble. I've already talked it over with Him, and He told me I shouldn't."

We smiled and replied, "Well, then, you have the answer, don't you?"

"Yes, I do," she said.

How, then, can people be brought to a decision? "He," the Holy Spirit, "will reprove . . . of sin" (John 16:8). "Having brought conviction of sin, and presented before the mind the standard of righteousness, the Holy Spirit withdraws the affections from the things of this earth, and fills the soul with a desire for holiness."—*The Acts of the Apostles*, pp. 52, 53. Who is it that fills the soul with a desire for holiness? It is the *Holy Spirit*. Let *me* not take *His* place and try to do *His* work. Let me be merely a channel through whom Jesus can speak.

6

THE BETTER METHOD

I had the privilege some time ago of talking with a man who had recently become a Christian. He is a leading officer in the county where he lives. He has a pleasing personality, and is a noble-appearing man. We had just built a new church in a city near his home, and he had come out to look it over. He thought perhaps there was something he could do to help us.

As he was about to leave I said, "Let me ask you a question, brother. Do you mind telling me what it was that caused you to take your stand for Christ?"

And then I thought I would prompt him so he would say what I wanted him to. I wanted to tell his story in my revival work. I thought it would help others. So I said, "Did your wife nag you a bit?" And I hoped he would say, "No." But he did not say anything.

I pressed him a bit, "Did she scold you a little, or nag you a bit?" And he just looked at me. Finally he shook his head slowly and continued to look meditatively.

I prompted him further, "You mean she did not scold you a little, or urge you a bit, or anything like that? Tell me, what did she do? I would like to know. I would like to tell others how men like you accept Christ."

He still stood there very thoughtfully. Finally he began, "Well, I will tell you. My wife did not scold me. She did not nag me. She was very good to me. But many a night I was awakened at midnight. I did not hear a word, only a muffled sob by the bedside. As I opened my eyes, and became accustomed to the darkness of the night, I saw the form of my wife kneeling there by the bed, softly sobbing her heart out to God. And I knew she was praying for me. That happened many, many, many times. And that is what brought me to Jesus."

82

Let us be careful in our soul-winning efforts always to let the Holy Spirit do the *impressing*. That is *His* work. *Ours* is to dramatize Jesus, even as He did the Father.

"If that is the way to win souls, then I have done it wrong all my life," lamented a Christian woman. She had tried only argument, denunciation, and condemnation. Of course she had by this method won no one to Christ. Jesus invites us, "Come . . . learn of me; for I am meek and lowly in heart" (Matt. 11:28, 29).

TWENTY-SIX MISUNDERSTANDINGS SETTLED

One woman, before her baptism, asked me to go with her to straighten out some misunderstandings she had had with her neighbors. I agreed. But when the hour arrived that I was to meet her at the church she was not there. Some moments later, however, she came walking briskly up the driveway. She was breathless, and I could see she had been hurrying.

"Pastor Coon," she said, "I am sorry I am late. But I got to thinking this thing over. I said to myself, 'Brother Coon did not have a part in my misunderstandings. Then why should he have to help me clear them up?' So I went out early this morning and started straightening things up."

I think she had apologized to, and made wrongs right with, twenty-six people since I had seen her last. She was very happy. And the Lord did a great work in that community. Jesus promised, "By this shall all men know that ye are my disciples, if ye have love one to another" (John 13:35).

It takes a big man to apologize. It takes real Christianity. It is no small, pygmy's job. But confession is the way to forgiveness and cleansing. It is also a great testimony to the world. It is powerful proof of the sincerity and humility of those who profess Jesus.

The strongest argument that can be produced in favor of Christianity "is a *loving* and *lovable* Christian." "By this shall all men know that ye are my disciples, if ye have love one to another" (John 13:35).

WHY SHE JOINED THE CHURCH

Years ago I was visiting with a woman whom it was my privilege to baptize. I asked her what it was that caused her to make her decision for Christ. I really expected her to mention some certain sermon that I had preached that had called for a real decision in her life—that had a degree of logic or very clear argument.

But imagine my surprise when she replied, "It was not any particular sermon you preached. It was your loving church."

Jesus said, "By this shall all men know that ye are my disciples, if ye have love one to another" (John 13:35).

A LOVE EXPERIENCE

Several years ago we organized a new church in a Southern city. The congregation had outgrown its building. We had two hundred charter members in this new organization. But we had no money with which to build a church—not even enough to purchase a lot. So the group started with nothing.

We needed a place in which to worship until we could build our own edifice. So we asked the Lord to provide us a place in which to meet. And the answer came when the beautiful Methodist church was opened to us by its pastor and Board of Stewards.

The pastor of that church was a wholesome Christian, and humble too. One morning as I was preaching I saw this good man sitting in the congregation. At the close of the service he shook my hand warmly and said, "Brother

Coon, I gained a victory this morning while you were preaching—a victory over discouragement.

"By the way," he continued, "will you preach for me some Sunday?"

"I shall be happy to," I replied, and then added, "Will you preach for me some Sabbath?"

"Yes," he agreed. And we exchanged pulpits on several occasions. And my constant prayer was that all of us who were meeting in that beautiful church might reveal Jesus, rather than resort to unkind criticism. I longed that we might uplift the Lamb of God before our Methodist brethren; even as they had represented Him in granting us a place in which to worship until we could build our own church.

At the beginning of our friendship we gave their Board of Stewards a banquet. We felt that if we did this to begin with, maybe it would be easier for them to forgive some poor church member who might indulge in a little argument or denunciation.

After eighteen months' stay in the Methodist church, we had purchased our lot and erected part of our structure. So we decided to move into our own building. We had no windows or doors yet. The seats were improvised from two-inch planks supported by concrete blocks. I told my good friend, the pastor of the Methodist church, "We have decided to move into our own building, rough though it is. I wish we could have a leave-taking service at which time we could express our appreciation to you and your gracious people for your kindness to us. But we have no place suitable for such a service."

"Come over to our church next Sunday morning," the gracious pastor replied. "We will have a leave-taking service in our sanctuary. You preach," he continued, "and I will preach. We will each take ten minutes. Half the choir will be from your group, and half from ours. Half the elders on the rostrum will be yours, and half ours. And would you ask your college to supply the special music?"

"All right," I agreed, "that will be wonderful!"

So when the day arrived, our congregation and his were sitting together. The gracious pastor asked me to take the first ten minutes of the preaching service.

"I am taking my text from Ephesians 2:4-6, 'God . . . hath . . . made us sit together.'" Thus I began my remarks. "I wish to give a double testimony this morning —first concerning our Methodist friends; and second, concerning Jesus. I love the Methodist people. My mother came from a very fine Methodist family."

Then I related how when I was a boy selling Christian literature to earn a scholarship, a very fine Methodist woman had opened her home to me one evening when I was very weary and hungry. She was most cordial and friendly, and made me feel right at home. And I thanked God for that dear Methodist woman. She was the answer to my prayer that evening.

Then I spoke of a time later in life when I was very ill. Many friends sent sympathy cards and greetings to me. But one of the most prized of all these was a greeting from a Methodist pastor of that city.

Then I spoke of how, when we were looking for a church in which to house our congregation until we could build, it was the Methodist people who came to our rescue.

In their usual graciousness, they opened the doors of their sanctuary to our use.

"You know," I said, "it is not hard for me to love the Methodist people. It just comes naturally to me, for the Methodists have been the answer to many a prayer."

"The next part of my testimony," I continued, "is concerning Jesus." And I mentioned a bit of what Jesus means to me. "In my sinfulness, He is my Saviour. In my weakness, He is my strength. In my ignorance, He is my wisdom." And I endeavored to picture my love for my Lord. I closed with the following lines I had penned that morning:

> He is altogether lovely
>   When days are glad and free;
> Perfumed with heaven's beauty,
>   The rose of sharon He.
>
> He is altogether lovely;
>   No night can ever bar
> The coming of His presence,
>   The bright and morning Star.
>
> He is altogether lovely;
>   My Lord will ever be
> The center of attraction
>   Throughout eternity.

As I was speaking I saw tears in the Methodists' eyes. It was because they loved Jesus. The Holy Spirit was present. We could *feel* Him there.

As I sat down the Methodist minister took the pulpit. "I take my text this morning from Hebrews 13:2: 'Be not forgetful to entertain strangers: for thereby some have entertained angels unawares.'

"Less than two years ago the Adventists came to our church as strangers. But now to us they are like angels.

"Ladies and gentlemen," he said, "up until two years ago I knew why God had raised up the Baptist people. It was to preach the great principle of the separation of church and state." Then he went on to mention various denominations and the special work God had given each to do, the purpose for which they had come into existence.

87

"But," he continued, "I must admit that up until two years ago, for the life of me, I could not figure out what in the world God had raised up the Adventists for. But during the last two years I have learned why God brought them into existence. God raised up the Seventh-day Adventist people," he cried, "to herald to the world the truth that God has a holy day! 'Remember the sabbath day, to keep it holy.' I want to tell you, my friends," he said, "this world needs to get back to Sabbathkeeping." In his very charitable manner, he allowed that it might be Saturday or Sunday. But his point was that God had raised up the Adventist people to bring the world back to God's holy Sabbath day.

Then he said, "Now another thing I have learned. Up until two years ago, I thought the Adventists' diet was merely a legalistic tenet. But I have learned that it is based on a broad principle of the Holy Scriptures. And that is, 'Your body is the temple of the Holy Ghost.' I have learned that that is why the Adventists eat as they do. O friends," he exclaimed, "there are some of you, members of my church, who are today spending more money on liquor, and tobacco, and other stimulants, than you are on God and His church. I am here to tell you this morning that the *only* stimulant that I can recommend that leaves no ill aftereffects is the *Holy Spirit.*

"Yes," he said, "we entertained the people whom we thought were strangers less than two years ago. But today they are to me like angels."

He closed his ten-minute talk and sat down. We sang together our closing song, "Blest be the tie that binds our hearts in Christian love!" While we were singing, I could *feel* the Spirit of the Lord there. And there were tears in many eyes throughout the congregation.

When the meeting was over I stepped around back

and shook hands with the Methodist pastor's wife. I said, "You folks have been most gracious to us."

She looked me full in the face as she shook my hand and said, "*We* have been the learners."

"But," I insisted, "you have been *so* gracious, Sister _____."

"I tell you, Brother Coon," she declared again, "*we* have been the learners. My husband just *started* to tell his congregation the wonderful things he knows about Adventists. There is so much more he *wanted* to say. He thinks you folks are wonderful."

Friends, I believe that those Methodists acted as Christ would have, don't you? They were so courteous and kind, and expressed "deference" toward us.

I heard that at least one Methodist woman went home that morning and called on the telephone a friend who had not been there. She said, "You should have been in church today. Something happened that you never heard of before. The Adventist preacher came down to our church and preached a Methodist sermon. And our Methodist preacher gave an Adventist sermon."

Do you think that that service just *happened? No! Never!* It was the harvest of a mutual love between the pastor of that church and the pastor of the Adventist church. It was a natural climax to a fellowship in Christ of two congregations who were far apart, doctrinally speaking, but made close through Jesus. *Jesus* is the one who binds hearts together in Christian love and fellowship.

"The strongest argument in favor of the gospel is a loving and lovable Christian." And "by this shall all men know that ye are my disciples, if ye have love one to another."

To be known as a Seventh-day Adventist is not enough. I want to be known first of all as a Christian, don't you? To know every recognized doctrine, merely, will not do. There is a *bigger* doctrine than all else beside. There is a telling argument that everyone of us *can* and *must* use—and that is Jesus and His love. Jesus in our lives. Jesus in our studies. Jesus in our homes. Jesus in our spirit. Jesus everywhere, and in everything we do and say. Thus the world will know that we are His disciples. And with Jesus living His life in us, we may humbly declare with Him, "He that hath seen me hath seen the Father" (John 14:9).

So let our prayer ever be:

> Lord, make me a nail upon the wall,
> Fastened securely in its place.
> Then from this thing so common and so small
> Hang a bright picture of Thy face
> That travelers may pause to look
> Upon the loveliness depicted there,
> And passing on their weary ways,
> Each radiant face may bear—
> Stamped so that nothing can efface—
> The image of Thy glory and Thy grace.
> Lord, let not one soul think of me.
> Only let me be a nail upon the wall,
> Holding Thy picture in its place.

"It was on the earth that the love of God was revealed through Christ. It is on the earth that His children are to reflect this love through blameless lives. Thus sinners will be led to the cross, to behold the Lamb of God."—*The Acts of the Apostles,* p. 334.

Jesus — Not Condemnation

~~~~~~

I GREW UP in a country of severe winters, where the snow often piles into deep drifts. We lived on a high hill. During those long winters we often had to go down into the valley below. We could have easily lost our way, for the road was completely covered with deep, drifting snow. To avoid this, some neighbors conceived a good idea. They cut down small trees, trimmed off the branches, and made stakes of them. Then between the road and the ditch they drove a stake on one side, and a stake on the other side. As the snow drifted deeper and still deeper, the outline of the road was completely wiped out. We could not see a trace of it. But we *could* see those stakes. Thus, no matter how deep the snow was, or how high the drifts, we could always stay in the middle of the road and avoid getting into either ditch.

Jesus, in His dealings with sinners, drives *stakes* to keep us from losing the way. On one side of the road he drives a great principle, "Neither do I condemn thee" (John 8:11). That is stake number one. That is to keep us from falling into the ditch of condemnation. And then, so that we will not go to the other extreme, the other

91

ditch, Jesus drives another stake, "Go, and sin no more" (John 8:11). This keeps us from upholding sin. Between these two stakes—"Neither do I condemn thee," and "Go, and sin no more"—is the road, the Way—Jesus.

Jesus does not want His followers to condemn the sinner. Neither does He want us to uphold him in his sin. Both are extreme positions. Neither one is the way. But between the two is Jesus. And He points to Himself, declaring, "I am the *way*" (John 14:6).

Suppose I go to a sinner and say, "You have brought disgrace on your family. You have shamed your wife and children." Does that help him any? Not at all.

Then, reporting on this "missionary" visit, I say, "I gave him something to think about. I certainly did!" What did I give him to think about? Discouragement! *Discouragement!* I did not do a bit of good to the poor man's soul. Not a bit! I only told him what he already knew. And doubtless the devil had been telling him the same thing for a long time. Probably the devil had been whispering in his ear, "You are a hypocrite. You are a cheat."

Then I came along and seconded the devil's motion. Then I made another mistake, that of reporting it as a missionary visit for the *Lord,* when it was actually a visit for the *devil.* Isn't that right? "God sent not his Son into the world to condemn the world; but that the world through him might be saved" (John 3:17).

John 3:16 is one of the great key texts of the Bible. This is a beautiful verse and tells us *why* God sent Jesus into this world. "For God so loved the world, that he gave his only begotten Son, that whosoever believeth in him should not perish, but have everlasting life." Yes, that verse tells us *why* God sent His Son into the world.

But John 3:17 follows immediately: "For God sent not

his Son into the world to condemn the world; but that the world through him might be saved."

When the woman taken in adultery was brought to Jesus, and after all her accusers were silenced, Jesus said, "Where are those thine accusers? hath no man condemned thee? She said, No man, Lord. And Jesus said unto her, Neither do I condemn thee." Was the woman worthy of condemnation? Yes. Had she done wrong? Yes. Was she a sinner? Yes. Was she an adulteress? Yes. Was she worthy of death? Yes. And yet Jesus said, "Neither do I condemn thee." I do not *condemn* you (John 8:10, 11).

A sinner is a spiritual convict. What a civil convict behind the prison bars wants is "out." Scolding will not get him out. Neither will condemnation. What he needs is the *key*. Give him the *key,* and he will get out all right.

We are all spiritual criminals in the prison house of sin. But Jesus said He came to open the prison house, and let the oppressed go free. He does not condemn the contrite one. He does not denounce the brokenhearted. He sets the longing captive free. *Jesus* is the *way.* He is the *key* to man's release.

OTHER METHODS

I believe "the Lord wants His people to follow other methods than that of condemning wrong, even though the condemnation is just."—*Gospel Workers,* p. 373. If I see a crook, I have no right to go around the community publishing the fact that he is crooked. My business is *not* to *expose* dishonest men, but to *reveal a Saviour.* There is a great deal of difference between the two. God does not authorize Christians to expose sinners, but to reveal the One who is "altogether lovely." I can expose evil men all my life long, and yet *not save* one of them. This is a crooked old world. But if I will show sinners the

"Way," some at least will look to Jesus and be saved. "The Lord wants His people to follow other methods than that of condemning wrong, even though the condemnation is just."

The woman of Samaria had had five husbands. And the man with whom she was then living was not her husband. But she was then looking into the face of a Saviour, who at that moment was cleansing her from sin. There is such a thing as the gospel erasing the past life. Wonderful fact! I have heard people today say, "Why, that man has three living wives." Jesus did not say that. I like the way He put it, don't you? He said, "You *have* had." Jesus was careful to let people know there is such a thing as "the land of beginning again." He did not *condemn.* Neither did He *uphold* people in sin.

I have noticed that the evil one has a plan that he follows. Someone in the church falls a prey to his temptations. Then the devil gets some person in the church to condemn him. You see, the *condemner* gets into one ditch. Then the devil gets another church member to look at the *condemner.*

Then this second church member says, "Isn't it *terrible!* That man condemns people! Terrible! Why doesn't he leave that poor man alone?"

Then the second man goes to the sinner and says, "You're all right!" And thus he goes to the extreme of upholding the sinner in his sin. And the devil sits back and laughs at them *both.* Both the first and the second man have missed Christ's method in dealing with that sinner. One has denounced the sinner. The other has upheld sin. Christ said, "Neither do I condemn thee." Stake *one!* "Go, and sin no more." Stake *two!* Between the two stakes is Jesus. And Jesus is the *way.*

One of the outstanding characteristics of Jesus and

His attitude toward sinners is His *balance*. He *never* went to extremes. Jesus gave to the world a *balanced* gospel. A gospel that does not condemn, and a gospel that shows the sinner the *way out*, is the gospel of Jesus. And I love Him for it, don't you?

A PERSONAL EXPERIENCE

I think I should not ask your pardon for the following personal experience. When we present principles to others, they have a right to know whether we are applying those principles ourselves.

We have a daughter. Her name is Juanita. At one time in her experience she went through a stage of life that all normal girls pass through. She liked the boys. They looked pretty good to her. (Now some of us older ones smile, because that never happened to us, you know!) And it began to frighten us, because we were afraid she might like the looks of some boy *too* much. You parents know how it is. So I began to scold her, in an effort to keep her from doing wrong. I began to take a condemning attitude toward her. Oh, of course I tried to be nice. You know how we like to salve our consciences, don't we? I tried to make myself believe I was being very nice about it all. But really, I was not too kind.

Then I thought of how I had often showed a drunkard how he could use the A B C method of taking a Bible promise, and have victory. A—is Ask (Matt. 7:7). B—is Believe (Mark 11:22-24). C—is Claim (1 Cor. 15:57). I have seen drunkards receive instantaneous victory over drink. I had just come from a revival, where in one ten-day series, several drunkards had gained complete victory over that enslaving habit. Many tobacco addicts had been released also.

I had explained to them: "Put your hand on a Bible

promise for victory. Then 'ask' God to give you victory. That is the 'A.' Then 'believe.' Say, 'I believe, through Jesus Christ, that God is giving me victory.' That is the 'B.' Then 'claim' what God has promised—claim victory in Jesus Christ now! That is the 'C.' " They did it. It worked! And they were delivered.

But then I returned to our lovely little daughter who needed help. And I was not taking a Bible promise and claiming wisdom to aid her. So I decided to do just that. I said, "God helping me, I will never condemn my daughter again as long as I live. I am going to my Lord and claim His promise. Has He not said in Isaiah 49:25, 'I will contend with him that contendeth with thee, and *I will save* thy children' ? "

So I said, "Lord, I ask You to save my daughter." That was the "A." "And I believe You *are* saving her." That was the "B." "I believe You are fulfilling Your word. For heaven and earth shall pass away, but Your word cannot fail. And I claim it through Jesus Christ. And I thank You for doing it." That is the "C"—just to claim all that God has promised, and thank Him for it.

What do you suppose happened just because I began to turn from the attitude of condemnation? I had not gotten *all* the meanness out of my blood yet. But I was a little sweeter to her. The more I claimed the promise of God, the more I was determined to stop condemning my poor, innocent little girl. I decided it was time for me to stop condemning entirely. I continued claiming Bible promises. And I reaffirmed my faith that He was fulfilling His word.

REWARDED

It was only a few days later that my daughter came to me with, "Daddy, you know, I have made a decision. None of this mushy stuff for me!"

And the Lord said to me, "Coon, be careful now. Don't *you* take the credit for this change. The credit belongs to her—not to you! So be careful!" Such a mistake on my part could ruin the whole program, couldn't it? Isn't it amazing how we try to take the credit for someone else's decision?

And so I said, "Wonderful! You are wonderful!" And she was—when I got out of the way and gave God and her a chance. "You know," I went on, "I am going to make a prediction for you. You are going to rate the friendship of the best boys on this college campus. You watch! The first you know they will want a **girl** who has such very high standards."

A few evenings later a young man saw her home. They were standing on the front steps. Finally, as he said good night, he wanted to kiss her wrist when they parted. "Oh, no!" she said, "I don't approve of that."

"That would be all right," he protested.

"Yes," she replied, "but it will be all right not to also." And he didn't.

When she told us about it, I said, "Wonderful! You're wonderful!" I could have said, "O Juanita, that is what *I* have been hoping for years. *I* have been hoping for this." I could have taken all the credit to myself. Instead of taking any credit to myself, I had better say, "God forgive me! I have been hindering by my condemning attitude. Now that I have changed, I have given God and my daughter a chance." Isn't that right? So I smiled and said, "Wonderful!" And I added, "The best young men on the college campus will be eager for your friendship."

CONFIDED IN ME

A few weeks later she and I were walking across the campus together. We saw a fine, noble-looking young man coming our way. He was a theological student who had just arrived from California. I had noticed him a few times myself, and admired him. As we saw him coming she said to me in a low, confidential tone, "Daddy, do you think I could land him?"

You see, now she was confiding in me because I did not condemn her. When she saw I was not denouncing her, she wanted to share her confidence with me. When I began to commend instead of condemn, she felt I was her friend. It is just that simple.

To her question I replied, "I think you could. But I want you to know something. I'm going to mind my own business. If you 'land him,' you'll land him alone, unless you want me to help you. And if there is something you want me to do, just let me know."

Ah, she liked that. She knew that daddy had begun to understand. Then she *wanted* me to help her. Isn't that wonderful! And that is the way it works.

A little later she asked her mother and me if we would like to invite that fine young fellow to dinner. "Surely," we said. So mother and daddy invited him to dinner. Of course mother and Juanita prepared the dinner, while daddy did the heavy looking on!

And she "landed him." Well, I wouldn't say it just that way. It proved that he was even more anxious to win her than she was to be won. Actually, both were cautious, considerate, and prayerful. And they are a happy couple today.

"Daddy and Mother," she wrote some time after they were married, "we have learned to claim the Bible promises. Oh," she said, "it is wonderful to put your hand on the promise God has given, and know He will fulfill His promise to you. Daddy and Mother, it works!" And now they are teaching other young people how to claim the promises of God for whatever problem is theirs.

I thank God that I stopped condemning, and began to commend her instead. My friends, it works. It really works! "God sent not his Son into the world to condemn the world; but that the world through him might be saved." *That* is why Jesus came. It was to show us the way.

WHAT KIND OF COMFORTERS?

When Job was having his trouble he said to the men who came to see him, "You are *'miserable comforters.'*" I am afraid that people would have to say that of us at times, aren't you? "Miserable comforters."

Then there is David. He got into trouble too. The Lord said to him, "Which do you prefer: to fall into the hands of man, or of God?"

David replied, "By all means, let me fall into the hands of the Lord. Don't let me fall into the hands of man." He could not trust man. Man might condemn him, but he knew God would pity him and have mercy upon him.

This leads me to believe that "the inhumanity of man toward man is our greatest sin. Many think that they are representing the justice of God, while they wholly fail of representing His tenderness and His great love. Often the ones whom they meet with sternness and severity are under the stress of temptation. Satan is wrestling with these souls, and harsh, unsympathetic words discourage them, and cause them to fall a prey to the tempter's power."— *The Ministry of Healing,* p. 163.

WRESTLING WITH SATAN

The human soul is wrestling with someone. With whom is he wrestling? The devil. They are in a life and death struggle. Then *I* appear on the scene. I see the poor soul is struggling hard. It is a terrific battle. But very heartlessly I say, "What's the matter with you? What are you carrying on like that for? Why don't you behave yourself?" I immediately discourage him. He loses his hold on his enemy. The battle is over. The poor soul is lost. The devil has won. That human being is now a lost soul, a plaything of the devil.

Before *I* came into the picture, he was almost victorious. But he lost his hold because *I* condemned him. And he fell a prey to the tempter's power. But *who* was responsible for the fall? *I* was.

Now let us take another look at these two wrestlers. The human soul is struggling with the evil one. He has a hold, but it is slipping. I again come into the picture. I immediately take in the situation. And with tenderness and love that is born from above I lay hold of the enemy and say, "Brother, by God's help we'll make it. Just another blow or two, brother, and that giant will be a defeated foe. Courage, brother, courage! God is with us." He takes fresh courage. He renews the struggle, and is victorious!

Now the battle is over. Our great enemy lies helpless on the ground. My brother and I stand there surrounded by angels from glory. He is victorious through Christ and the confidence that I expressed in him during the struggle.

What was it that made the difference? Instead of condemning my brother, I went to his rescue. I stood by his side and encouraged him. I helped him to get his hand in the hand of his Saviour, who *never* lost a battle.

How I Failed

Don't become discouraged. If you have used wrong methods in soul winning, so have I. If you are guilty, I am more so.

Several years ago I was pastor of a district of churches in which there was an academy about eighteen miles distant. One morning my telephone rang, and the business manager of the academy begged me to come over at once. He said, "I am in trouble. Please help me out."

I jumped into my car and went as fast as I dared to. When I arrived I learned that my friend was on the second floor. So up I went. As I walked into the room, there I saw the business manager and a woman. And this woman was giving him the tongue lashing of his life. My, how I pitied him! I really felt extremely sorry for that poor fellow.

And you know, all at once, my righteous indignation was aroused. That is what *we* call it—righteous indignation. I think God may have another word for it. I sensed the woman was in the wrong by the spirit she manifested. So I imbibed a bit of the same spirit.

After listening awhile, I spoke. "Do you know what I would do if I were you?" speaking to the business manager. "I wouldn't even stay in this room with this woman." What was I doing?—condemning her. And she heard it. But the business manager was happy for the counsel.

Under Conviction

And so in another moment we were on our way down the stairway. We were about halfway down the first flight of steps when the Lord caught up with me. I had gotten ahead of the Lord, you see. You know, one can do that. The Lord was saying to me, "Coon, you have condemned. That is not the gospel of Jesus. That is not Christ's way."

I turned to the business manager right there on the stairway and exclaimed, "Brother, I have made a mistake. I gave you poor counsel."

"I think you gave me good counsel," he replied. "I am going to take it." And I began to think he was going to take two steps at a time the rest of the way down!

Again I exclaimed, "Brother, I have made a mistake. I must return."

"If you go back," he replied, "you're going alone."

And then I thought to myself, "Oh, I wish I could blank out just that one sentence I spoke up there in that room." Just *one* sentence! That is all it was. Oh, if I had not said *anything*. But I had. And I was thinking that before I had said that *one* sentence the controversy was between the business manager and the woman. I was sitting there very contentedly. *Then* I was only a listener. But the moment I made that *one* statement, *he* was released. And now *I* had an account to settle.

Then I remembered some good counsel I had received years before. It was that I am to apologize to another as though I were the *chief* offender, whether I really am or not. Even though the other person may be *twenty times* as guilty as I, I am to apologize as though I were the chief offender.

I Repented

I called, "Well, brother, I am going back up."

I believe that was about the hardest set of stairs I have ever climbed in my life. And I asked God to help me. I had condemned, and I must make it right with the woman.

So I went on up to the room where we had been. And, bless your heart, the woman had moved on up to another floor. Then Satan said to me, "Oh, you've done enough now. It isn't necessary to walk up another flight."

But I said, "I'll go on up. God give me the strength." But that *was* the hardest flight of stairs I ever had to climb. It seemed I could hardly put one foot ahead of the other. But I determined to keep on going. I climbed step after step, with the constant prayer in my heart that God would help me. I knew I could never face that woman alone. I *must* have divine help.

Friends, I have discovered that it is much easier to

102

condemn than it is to apologize. But God commands, "Confess your faults one to another" (James 5:16).

Finally I reached the top of the stairs, and found the woman in a little room in the attic. And you should have seen the look she gave me!

THE APOLOGY

"Sister," I began, "I have come up to apologize to you for what I said. I want you to forgive me."

"Well," she retorted, "how sorry are you?" And, oh, the look she gave me!

It put me in mind of the way one of our cats at home used to play with a mouse. She would not quite kill it, but neither would she let it go. And that was the way that woman was handling me. So I prayed in my heart, "Lord, help me to take it. Help me to take it! It is coming to me. I condemned. But now I have to straighten it out."

So I said, "Sister, I am *very* sorry. And I hope you will forgive me."

"Are you sure? Are you *sure?*" Then she gave me a kind of "new look." And she went on punishing me with sarcasm. I do not know how long she went on like that, but it seemed a long time to me.

Finally I said kindly, "Sister, I do not know what the burden of your heart is. But I know there must be a great burden there. And I know that only God can take it away." I do not remember the exact words I used, but in effect I said, "I am sorry that I have condemned you. I should have been praying for you and helping you to bear your burden. I have come up now to pray for you, and with you. And I wonder if you would let me pray with you now."

She just sat there and looked at me for a few more

103

seconds. And then she said, "Well, O.K., if you are sure you mean it."

We smile now, but it was not funny then. So we both knelt there on that attic floor.

I talked to the Lord from the depths of my heart. And as I did so, I felt the warmth of His Holy Spirit. Do you know why I did? The change was in *me*. I had changed from the spirit of condemnation to one of trying to help someone. And the Lord could do something with me, and for me, and through me then. I felt His Spirit filling my soul. I was doing more than praying audibly. I was praying *in my heart* for that dear woman. Really I was. My own heart was changed.

When I closed my prayer this woman prayed. And such a prayer I have never heard in all my life. She broke down and wept. She sobbed, "Lord, I want to tell You now in the hearing of this preacher that I am to blame for everything that has happened." And then she went on and described to the Lord, and me, the details of the affair, and how *she* was at the bottom of all the trouble.

And that dear woman gave her heart to Jesus in reconsecration right there on her knees on that attic floor. By my turning from the path of condemnation, God graciously used me to save that dear soul. And by my example, I actually taught her how to apologize.

Yes, the Bible commands us, "Confess your faults one to another, and pray one for another." The world today is confessing the other man's faults, and talking about him, instead of confessing its own faults and praying for the other fellow. It makes all the difference in the world which we do. I should be out confessing *my own* faults and *praying* for the other man, instead of confessing *his faults* and *defending* myself.

"God sent not his Son into the world to condemn the world; but that the world through him might be saved" (John 3:17).

WHY WE SHOULD NOT CONDEMN

"Most pitiable is the condition of him who is suffering under remorse; he is as one stunned, staggering, sinking into the dust. He can see nothing clearly. The mind is beclouded, he knows not what steps to take. Many a poor soul is misunderstood, unappreciated, full of distress and agony,—a lost, straying sheep. He can not find God, yet he has an intense longing for pardon and peace.

"O, let no word be spoken to cause deeper pain! To the soul weary of a life of sin, but knowing not where to find relief, present the compassionate Saviour."—*The Ministry of Healing,* p. 168.

Here is the picture of a man who is frustrated, confused, stunned. And he does not know what to do. He wants to do right, but he cannot find the next step to take. He needs a Christian friend to aid him. We should not say, "Brother, you are doing right," when he is not. Oh, no! We should never defend a sinner in his sin. Never! But we should go to his side in the spirit of Christ, and say, "Brother, Jesus loves you and me. And if you are guilty of *this* sin, I may be guilty of a worse sin. If you have made mistakes, I may have made greater mistakes. Now, here is Jesus. Jesus is bending over us. He loves us, and He will see us through." That is the gospel of Jesus Christ that He has commissioned us to carry.

I pray that God may help me not to condemn anyone any more. What do you say? O how many times I have failed! May God forgive us all! I pray God that I will present the lovely Saviour so the heart that is lost and straying will see where to take the next step, and the

105

next step, and still the next, until he finally falls at the foot of the cross in deep repentance.

AMAZING DISCOVERY

Some time ago I came across a Bible study that caused me to get down on two knees before God and plead for His pardon. It amazed me beyond measure. And this is what it was. It is very simple. And it shows from the Bible that he who condemns another, or he who gossips about another, or he who judges his brother's motives, is guilty of three sins. Let me share this study with you.

First, the man who condemns, or judges, the motives of his brother, is guilty of the *same* sin. "Thou art inexcusable, O man, whosoever thou art that judgest: for wherein thou judgest another, thou condemnest thyself; for thou that judgest doest the same things" (Rom. 2:1).

Even though I have not committed the *act* of which I judge my brother to be guilty, the fact that I judge him, and condemn him for that sin, shows that if the opportunity presented itself, under the proper conditions, and with favorable circumstances, *I* would do the same thing of which I am accusing him. And God judges me, not by the act that I commit, but by what is in my heart that *would* come out if the opportunity were favorable. That is it, isn't it? Jesus said that the *thought* of evil is sin. "Whosoever looketh on a woman to lust after her hath committed adultery with her already in his heart" (Matt. 5:28). Although he has not committed the overt act, in God's sight the person who harbors the sin in his heart is still guilty of that sin.

So, if I condemn another brother, if I judge his motives, whether *he* is guilty or not—*I am*. Strong indictment, but true.

106

The Lord says that the second sin of which the condemner, the judger of the motives of others, is guilty is a much greater one than the first. And that sin is Pharisaism and hypocrisy. Jesus says, "Thou hypocrite" (Matt. 7:3-5).

So if I judge the motives of my brother, I am a hypocrite. I am guilty of Pharisaism and conceit. The very act of judging another builds up in my nature, and in my character, Pharisaism, self-righteousness, which in the sight of God is the most offensive of any sin.

But the enormity of condemning others is not seen until we study the third sin. When I read *that* one, it drove me to my knees. Here it is: "The Father . . . hath committed all judgment unto the Son" (John 5:22). God has given to His Son the chair of judgment. "All judgment." Not 80 per cent. Not 90 per cent. Not even 99 per cent. But *all* judgment is committed to the Son. *Christ* sits in the chair of judgment. Therefore, it says that he who assumes to take *that chair* is trying to take the place of Christ. And by that act he is committing the sin brought to view in 2 Thessalonians 2:3 and 4 of which the *antichrist* is guilty. And he is, by the act of trying to slip into the judgment seat of Christ, becoming *an associate of the antichrist.*

Next I read where the Scriptures declare that even now there are *"many antichrists"* (1 John 2:18). I had never in my life preached on *many* antichrists. I had told about *the* antichrist. And it was scriptural. I would not for a moment minimize the force of the great prophecy of the antichrist, the Papacy, who has thought to change God's unalterable law. What I had preached is *all* true. But *more* than that is true. The Bible says there are "many antichrists."

Summarizing: First, he who condemns another and

107

judges his brother's motives is guilty of the same sin of which he judges another. Second, he is guilty of a much greater offense, that of Pharisaism, of hypocrisy, censoriousness, conceit. Third, he is guilty of being an associate of the great antichrist, if not actually one of the "many" antichrists.

Do you know what I did? I got right down on my knees before God. I cried out, "God, spare Thy people! Spare professing Christians, O God, and forgive us of our sins! And, Lord, help me to carry *this* message to as many Christians as I can." I don't want to be an associate of the antichrist, or one of the many last-day antichrists, do you?

So our message must be Jesus—not condemnation. If Jesus, to whom all judgment has been committed, was not sent to condemn the world, then how can I, to whom *no* judgment has yet been committed, condemn anyone? "Let us not therefore judge one another any more: but judge this rather, that no man put a stumblingblock or an occasion to fall in his brother's way" (Rom. 14:13).

STUMBLING

Friend, if *you* are stumbling along toward the kingdom, do not become discouraged. And if you see another stumbling along, do not condemn him. Someday both you and he may pass through those pearly gates if you just keep on, always setting your face in the right direction. But since we have all stumbled so often along our Christian pathway, it ill behooves any of us to condemn some other sinner.

Some years ago there was a little baby girl born into our home. Her name was Juanita. And do you know, it seemed like months before that little girl could even creep. But after a while she started creeping around on the floor. Do you suppose her mother said, "Shame on you, you little good-for-nothing thing! *Crawling!*"

Oh, no! Oh, *no!* Mother was delighted to see such progress. "Daddy, come! Come, Daddy! Look! Juanita's making it. She can *creep.*" And the little darling would look up and smile, because she was getting some encouragement.

Before long she was able to put her hand on a chair and stand on her little chubby legs. But she was wobbly—oh, *so* wobbly. And of course *down* she went. Do you suppose I said, "Shame on you. Can't you even stand up holding on to a chair?" Oh, no! Of course not. I did nothing of the kind. I was delighted. She was making progress, you see.

Then finally she took her little hand off the chair and put one foot in front of the other. But *down* she went again. Did I say, "I'm ashamed of you! You started walking and have fallen so soon!" You're right, I didn't say that.

I said, "Wonderful, honey! Wonderful! Come on to daddy." And I stood there with outstretched arms to encourage her to come. "You're doing fine. Come on, darling. You'll make it!" And she got up and smiled so contentedly and started toward me again. And so she kept on.

And do you know—today that girl can walk all right!

If you set your face toward the kingdom of God, you may stumble, and stumble again. But keep looking to Jesus. And someday, through His wonderful grace, you will go through the gates into the city—the city of God. But as we travel along, let us never condemn another stumbling, struggling, confused soul. Let us rather be like Jesus. "For God sent not his Son into the world to condemn the world; but that the world through him might be saved."

Witnessing for Jesus

I DON'T BLAME Jim for leaving me," I heard Dorothy say sadly at the close of a study on soul winning. We had known Dorothy for a number of years. She was a very sincere Christian. She was also a faithful wife and devoted and loving mother. And in addition, Dorothy had earned much of the family's living for a number of years.

Dorothy had, however, made a mistake common to many earnest, conscientious Christians. She had scolded Jim for his mistakes and evil habits, instead of being only a witness for Jesus. Her condemning attitude, although perhaps much kinder than many others, still could not win a sinner to Christ. Dorothy had occasionally belittled Jim, preached at him, exhorted him, and criticized him.

However, this method had not led Jim to Christ. The Holy Spirit was now pointing out to Dorothy her mistake. She acknowledged her error, confessed her sin to God, and was forgiven.

ONLY A WITNESS

"Ye are my witnesses," God declares (Isa. 43:10, 12). And again Jesus commands, "This gospel of the kingdom shall be preached in all the world for a witness" (Matt. 24:14). If we could now step into a courtroom, with court in session, we would see the judge on his bench, the prosecuting attorney, the attorney for the defense, the jury, the witnesses, and the spectators. Each of these has his specific duties to perform. Each has his place. Each is an important office.

But in the spiritual court Jesus has assigned all His followers *one* office. And what is that? Are we prosecuting attorneys? No. Are we defense attorneys? No; we are not to defend sin. Are we members of the jury? No. Are we the judge? No. Are we merely spectators? No; we have a very definite part to play in God's plan. What are we then? "Ye are my witnesses," God says (Isa. 43:10, 12). That is it—just a witness.

When we realize the work God has assigned us is *witnessing,* a great burden is removed from our shoulders, isn't it? "Go home to thy friends, and tell them how great things the Lord hath done for thee, and hath had compassion on thee," was the command Jesus gave the healed demoniac (Mark 5:19). His business was to witness. That was all—just to be a *witness!*

However, Dorothy had not thought of soul winning in terms of witnessing; but rather of judging, scolding, condemning, nagging, and telling others where they were wrong. But Christ declares that *witnessing* is the method to be used in carrying the gospel to all the world (Matt. 24:14). What a beautiful picture is painted when we combine the word "gospel," or "good news," with the word "witnessing." Ah, it is a picture of Christians, followers of the meek and lowly Jesus, traversing land and sea, displaying to all they meet the beauty they have found in Jesus and the joy that is theirs in following the Master. A carrier of "good news" is quite different from a condemning, criticizing, denouncing, long-faced Christian, isn't he?

SEEKING COUNSEL

Some time ago Dorothy made a hundred-and-forty-mile trip to see my wife and me. "Brother Coon," she said, "I have come to seek counsel from you."

"That is fine," I replied. "Now, before we get into the subject, let me give you the first bit of counsel. It is from Jeremiah 17:5: 'Thus saith the Lord; Cursed be the man that trusteth in man.' So don't believe anything I tell you, unless I find it in the Bible."

"Well," she replied, "thank you. Now I *am* ready for counsel."

Then I added, "I have more counsel for you. This is found in James 1:5-8, where we are told: 'If any of you lack wisdom, let him ask of God.' Since God is the only One who can impart heavenly wisdom, if you should ask of *me* wisdom, and *I* should profess to give it to you, I would be attempting to make myself God! So why should *I* try to tell *you* what to do? I *do* have a right to outline principles from the Bible to guide you in making your decision. And that I shall do. But it is your God-given right to interpret those principles in your personal life. If I should try to do that, going into every detail and telling you exactly what you should do, I would be taking the place of God. And that is blasphemy (John 10:33)."

So we discussed Dorothy's problem with her. And, friends, a great load had been lifted from my shoulders. I did not feel it was my responsibility to tell her exactly what she was to do. There *was* a time when I thought it was my duty to tell a person exactly what he must do in almost any given case. But I have learned that is not true counseling.

I have also learned that the same Lord who is willing to reveal to *me my* duty is willing to reveal to the *other man his* duty. "We cannot depend for counsel upon humanity. The Lord will teach us our duty just as willingly as He will teach somebody else. If we come to Him in faith, He will speak His mysteries to us personally. . . . Those who decide to do nothing in any line that will displease God, will know, after presenting their case before Him, just what course to pursue. And they will receive not only wisdom, but strength. Power for obedience, for service, will be imparted to them, as Christ has promised."—*The Desire of Ages,* p. 668.

That lifts a tremendous burden from my shoulders. I am not the judge. I am not the prosecuting attorney. I am only the witness. That is what the Lord says. "Ye are my witnesses, saith the Lord" (Isa. 43:10, 12).

The mistake Dorothy made with Jim, I have also often made. I have scolded. I have belittled. I have embarrassed individuals. Now I have learned that those tactics belong to the prosecuting attorney, or perhaps even the attorney for the defense may direct such remarks to his opponent. But the witness? *Never!* The judge may be very sharp. The jurors may bring in a sentence that is severe. But *not* the *witness.* He merely tells what he has *seen,* what he *knows.* And God declares, "Ye are my witnesses" (Isa. 43:10, 12).

NOT MULE RELIGION

Sometimes we have had the idea that religion is a puritanical type of thinking. Some believe that to be religious means to be long-faced. But he who travels his religious life sighing, crying, and moaning, with his head bowed down like a bulrush, is not a witness of the glad tidings of the gospel. He is, rather, a false witness.

8

I heard a Baptist preacher tell the story of a little boy who attended a religious meeting and "got religion," as some people call it. Returning home from the service, the lad bounded into the house. He found his grandfather sitting in a chair.

"Grandfather, I've got religion," exclaimed the lad in great glee.

The grandfather belonged to a different school of thought. "If you've got religion, sit down and behave yourself," he demanded. But you know it is pretty hard for a boy to sit—just sit. If he can, he is different from me!

So the little boy tried to sit there. But he could not sit still. He had to wiggle. Pretty soon the cat came along. He picked up his little pet and put her on his lap. He stroked her for a while, and that gave a little vent to his wiggle. By and by the dog came up to him. He picked him up and put him on his lap too. Then the three of them—the boy, the cat, and the dog—had a good time together. But almost before the boy realized what he was doing—he was just wiggling his fingers, you know—he had tied together the tails of his two pets. And of course you know what happened then!

The old grandfather glared at the little boy and shouted, "Now see what you have done! Get out of here! Get out of here!"

The boy ran outside the house and stood by the barn. As he looked over the fence, he saw the mule in the barnyard. And the picture he got was one of the old mule stooped over a bit. One ear was lopped forward and the other backward. One eye sort of looked up and the other down. One front leg was forward and the other backward. And the lower lip was cupped as if ready to take the offering. The boy looked at that mule in amazement for a moment, then exclaimed, "Oh, I see! There's a Christian."

Well, you know, as I heard the Baptist preacher relate that story, I said to myself, "That's it. That's it!" That is the way many people have sized up Christianity because *we* have not borne a better witness. They think it makes a person *so sober* that he actually goes mourning all along the way to His Father's house. And some people think that religion is a funeral procession instead of a march. But religion is a march—a joyful march toward the kingdom of God. And I have a positive duty to let people know that Jesus Christ has made me happy.

I have a *duty* to let people know that the religion I have found makes me happier than the man who has not discovered it. Isn't that right? That *is* right. Jesus has made my heart light. And He has taken away the burden of judging. Oh, judging was a *big* burden. The burden of condemning, the burden of arguing, the burden of examining the other fellow—were all *so* heavy. *Now* as only a witness, I am happy and lighthearted. And I have every right to be joyful in Jesus.

Someone asks me, "Why do you keep Saturday?"

I can witness to the joy of it without condemning him for keeping another day. "I keep the seventh-day Sabbath because Jesus did. And He told me to keep it (Luke 4:16; Matt. 24:20). Keeping it makes me happier, and I love Jesus more for it." Do you know of any better reason? Jesus did it. He tells me to. And obeying Him makes me happier than if I did not. And that is enough to know, isn't it? Doesn't it make me happy? Yes, I *want* to do it. He told me to "call the sabbath a delight" (Isa. 58:13). I do not have to condemn anyone, or argue with him, or judge him. I am only a witness. When someone inquires concerning my faith, I can do as Peter says, "Be ready always to give an answer to every man that asketh you a reason of the hope that is in you with

115

meekness and fear" (1 Peter 3:15). Then Christ's "yoke is easy," and His "burden is light" (Matt. 11:30).

BIG TOYS!

A father and mother came to us awhile ago seeking advice on how to train their three small children. They were *very* anxious to rear them so they would love the Lord. When they asked us how we trained our children, it almost frightened us. We could think of plenty of mistakes we had made. But it was difficult to think of any good things we had done. What should we tell them? Finally my wife gave a few good suggestions. And then I said, "Well, I'll tell you one thing to do. Make religion *very* joyful."

"We are trying to make the Sabbath a different day," they said.

"Yes, indeed," I replied, "we want it to be a different day. But in what way? It is to be *delightfully* different; not *negatively* different." The Sabbath commandment begins with a positive assertion—not a negation: "Remember the sabbath day, to keep it holy" (Ex. 20:8). And God commands us to "call the sabbath a delight" (Isa. 58:13).

We might say, "Children, when Sabbath comes we are going to have something extra good for dinner."

And the children respond joyously, "Oh, goody, goody, goody! I can't wait for Sabbath to come. Mother is going to have something extra good for dinner. I can hardly wait!" Friends, we must make the Sabbath a "delight."

Then when Friday evening comes and the Sabbath hours are approaching, let us not say very solemnly and puritanically, "Sabbath is here. Now children, put away all your toys." Do you know what "toys" mean to children? When we say "toys," that means "fun." So if we say,

"Put away all your toys, Sabbath is almost here," it is just like saying: "Now we can't have any more fun. The Sabbath is coming. So put away all your fun." So to the children religion and the Sabbath are connected with "no more fun."

Instead of that, let us plan extra "fun" for the children on the Sabbath. Oh, no, I don't mean anything hilarious—not secular, but sacred "fun." Plan special toys for the Sabbath. In other words, special fun. Sabbath books, Sabbath puzzles, Sabbath games, Sabbath nature walks. And what can possibly be more fun than a Sabbath nature walk, with the trees, the birds, the flowers, or whatever nature has to offer in any particular season? And the lessons we can teach our children from nature are numberless. Lunch in the woods, or by a babbling brook, or in a grassy meadow on a beautiful Sabbath day is a memory the children will ever cherish. We know whereof we speak, because some of the most sacred memories of childhood Sabbaths center around just such fun.

"Children, Sabbath is almost here. Let's put away all our little toys and now we will have 'big toys!'" And what might they be? Something such as we use in the Sabbath school—the sand table with beautiful cutouts, Peter, James, John, Moses, and Jesus. And everything we can think of that will turn the minds of our children in a special sense to Jesus and His love, we should study to employ. Such things make religion joyful.

And the children will say, "Oh, Sabbath is coming! Mommy, how long will it be before Sabbath? I can hardly wait! We are going to have our 'big toys' and something extra good to eat, and just lots of fun."

When we give our children such a joyful conception of the Sabbath, that is truly witnessing for Jesus, because that is making religion beautiful.

117

We told our friends who came to us, "We have made many mistakes with our children. But one thing we were determined to do for them, and that was to make religion joyful. At times in our home I almost went to extremes of joy. I wanted our children to look upon religion as something pleasant, something to be desired. I did not want them to get the impression that a life with Jesus consists of negatives.

"Make worship time joyful and *short*. Instead of saying, 'Sit up straight now, Jesus is here,' we might better say, 'Let us sit quietly now so we can hear Jesus talking to us. If we are noisy, we can't hear Him. And then we want to talk to Jesus too.' " And then make the Scripture reading or the Bible story short and interesting. And let the prayers be short too, especially when the children are small. The time for *long* prayers is in our private devotions. Children should not be burdened with *long* prayers. That ruins the joy of the worship period.

Worship time should not be used as an occasion to scold or punish the children. Let *everything* that has *anything* to do with religion be *joyful*. And let us develop in the lives of our children a *happy* religion. "The *joy* of the Lord is your strength" (Neh. 8:10). "Rejoice in the Lord alway: and again I say, Rejoice" (Phil. 4:4).

We have a positive duty to witness to the world that we are happier than they because we have found Jesus. Then keen minds will desire our religion. But if religion consists of negatives merely, we should expect only legalists and dyspeptics and constitutionally sad and melancholy people to accept Jesus Christ and His truth. We repeat, "Rejoice in the Lord alway: and again I say, Rejoice." This is being a true witness for Jesus, when coupled with a consistent life of truthfulness, kindness, meekness, purity, obedience, wholesomeness, and delight.

If I take an attitude of condemnation, of judging, of selfishness, et cetera, I am a false witness. I deny my Lord with such an attitude. Christians "may deny Him by shunning life's burdens, by the pursuit of sinful pleasure. They may deny Him by conforming to the world, by uncourteous behavior, by the love of their own opinions, by justifying self, by cherishing doubt, borrowing trouble, and dwelling in darkness. In all these ways they declare that Christ is not in them. And 'whosoever shall deny Me before men,' He says, 'him will I also deny before My Father which is in heaven!' "—*The Desire of Ages*, p. 357.

A PREACHER FRIEND

"Brother, are you saved?" were almost the first words from the lips of a stranger who greeted me cordially as I was pulling into a trailer park.

And I thought, "My, what an argument I could put up on that!" I could have said, "Now, brother, what *tense* of salvation do you refer to—past, present, or future?"

But instead I replied, "Yes, sir, brother, I am." I felt quite sure what he really meant to ask me was, "Have you found Jesus? Has He saved you from sin?" And so I replied, "Yes, sir, brother, Christ is my personal Saviour. Praise the Lord." Then I added, "I am a preacher."

"Hallelujah," he exclaimed. "I want to tell you, the Lord Jesus has been wonderful to me. Once it was the bottle; now it is the Book!"

Friends, do you know what the preacher was doing, even though he was perhaps a little eccentric? He was witnessing to his Lord.

Still standing by the car, he asked, "What denomination?"

"Seventh-day Adventist," I replied. And I noticed his head drop a bit. And I thought, "Oh, it must be that at some time in his life some well-meaning church member has denounced or condemned him. And perhaps tried to argue a bit." But in spite of this temporary gulf, this preacher was very kind to me.

I was placed on a lot in the park right next to this preacher. And I resolved, by the help of the Lord, to be a good witness for our Lord. I decided not to force doctrine on him, but to let the love of Jesus shine out through me. I would just *love* him. Christ is not prejudiced against people of any denomination, so why should I be? Satan tempted me to ask this clergyman what denomination he represented, but I stoutly resisted. For after all, what difference did it make to me? I had already made up my mind just to *love* him and his wife, anyway. And I thought, "When Jesus comes again, He is going to decide who is worthy of heaven, not on the basis of denomination, but of character. So why should I give anyone the impression that denomination is the big thing, when I know it is not?"

My wife and I prayed together for that dear preacher and his wife. He kept everything around his trailer neat and attractive. And often as we saw him working on his lawn, we remarked to each other how we believed this good man truly loved the Lord, for he was always praising Him for His goodness. He and I would often see each other in the yard, and many times I dropped a word of confidence in him. One day I shook his hand and said, "Behold an Israelite indeed, in whom is no guile!" (John 1:47). And tears came to his eyes.

At another time I said, "We are pleased with the loving atmosphere of your life here in our camp." He smiled again, and once more I saw tears in his eyes. He was a little surprised, perhaps, to have a man of another faith say that to him. But he should not have been. For we all should be witnesses for Jesus in our *lives,* and not think that the presentation of any abstract doctrine will constitute us witnesses for Jesus.

"Our doctrines may be correct; we may hate false doctrine, and may not receive those who are not true to principle; we may labor with untiring energy; but even this is not sufficient. . . . A belief in the theory of the truth is not enough. *To present this theory to unbelievers does not constitute you a witness for Christ.*"—*Christ Our Righteousness,* pp. 78, 79.

One evening my wife was passing by the preacher's trailer home. A young couple were visiting them at the time. The door of the trailer was open, and my wife overheard them praying together. The preacher was praying in most earnest and sincere tones, "Lord, we are together in one accord. Lord, make us kind, make us sweet,——" And then she passed beyond the sound of his voice. Bless your heart, that preacher was witnessing to His precious Lord right there on his knees. He was asking for the sweetness of the character of Jesus. That is worth much. He was asking God to keep him kind. That is being like Jesus.

I am afraid that at times "the trouble with our work has been that we have been content to present a cold theory of the truth. How much more power would attend the preaching of the word today, if men dwelt less upon the theories and arguments of men, and far more upon the lessons of Christ, and upon practical godliness."—*Ibid.,* p. 79.

This preacher was asking God for a practical godliness. My wife and I had been pleading with God for the same. God wants His children to be wholesome Christians. If we fail in this, we are denying Jesus instead of witnessing for Him. What we need is a proper balance of what constitutes true Christianity.

Passing our friends' home one day, I paused a moment

121

to speak with him. I remarked, "As my wife and I look out of our window, we often say as we see you here, 'God bless him.' " Tears again filled his eyes.

Placing his big hand on my little shoulder, he said, "Brother, let us make a promise to each other. You pray for me, and I will pray for you."

"Let us do that," I agreed. And before I could speak another word, his head was bowed in prayer. He was inviting God to go with me and to go with him. We were both to move from that camp in a few days. As he prayed, I placed an arm about him. Then I gently patted him. In his prayer he said, "Lord, make us kind. Make us sweet. Help us to be like Jesus." And then he claimed a promise from the Word for each of us as we journeyed.

When he closed his prayer I prayed. I thanked the Lord for the fellowship we had had in Christ. I asked the Father to go with him and continue to aid him in his wonderful work for God. As I was praying I heard him sniffling. I knew he was weeping. But they were tears of fellowship. When he and his wife moved from the park, we bade them good-by. His wife remarked to my wife, "We have enjoyed so much being near you. We are one."

I liked the way that preacher witnessed for Jesus in our trailer park. He loved His Lord. There could be no question about that. And "if we are Christ's, our sweetest thoughts will be of Him. We shall love to talk of Him; and as we speak to one another of His love, our hearts will be softened by divine influences."—*The Desire of Ages,* p. 83.

Doubtless my preacher friend did not have the very best education. And his work was confined largely to criminals in our jails and penitentiaries. But "it is not always the most learned presentation of God's truth that convicts and converts the soul. Not by eloquence or logic are men's hearts reached, but by the sweet influences of the Holy Spirit, which operate quietly yet surely in transforming and developing character. It is the still small voice of the Spirit of God that has power to change the heart."—*Prophets and Kings*, p. 169.

JESUS A WITNESS

Jesus was born as a witness. "For this cause came I into the world, that I should bear witness unto the truth," declared Jesus (John 18:37). And He is our example. As He was in the world, so we are in the world. His works bore witness that He came from God (John 10:25). And He promises us, "But ye shall receive power, after that the Holy Ghost is come upon you: and ye shall be witnesses unto me" (Acts 1:8).

STEWARDSHIP

My wife and I have for years practiced tithing; that is, paying one tenth of our income into the church for the support of the gospel. Then we have also, for the most part, returned a second tithe or a bit more, in one form or another. We have a perfect right to share with others the blessings we receive in tithing.

To me, tithing is stewardship. At least it is an important part. We would not take a great deal for the blessings that come to us through this phase of stewardship. The answers to prayer we have received through claiming a stewardship promise (Mal. 3:10-12) are absolutely miraculous. We have received scores of wonderful answers to prayer through the blessings of faithful stewardship alone.

Now, as witnesses for Jesus, we may share these experiences with others. But we must stop short of condemning others for not tithing. What they do about it is be-

123

tween them and God alone. God is the Judge. We may even read what God tells us in Malachi 3:8, but we must be careful to let the Holy Spirit do the applying and impressing. Christ truly declared that His Word will judge us in the last day. And that is a serious matter. But I must let the Word do the judging. I must stay on the witness stand and not climb over into the judge's bench—no, not for even a moment.

WITNESSING IN DIET

In one church where a revival was being held, classes on soul winning were being conducted a half hour or so before the preaching service for the public. As the class was meeting in one section of the room, the guests were coming in for the next service.

Among those who came was a guest who had never entered an Adventist church until the opening revival meeting. But she attended night after night. She sat nearby and listened as this class study was being conducted. I noticed she seemed eager to hear what I was saying to the class. The last Sabbath morning when a call was extended for those who wished to join the church, this woman responded, and came down to the front.

A few days later the pastor and I visited her in her home to instruct her for baptism. In reviewing with her the doctrines of God's Word and Bible principles of Christian living, we finally came to the subject of diet. And we told her of the unclean meats, including swine's flesh, and other creatures that are pointed out in the Bible as being unhealthful because they are scavengers (Leviticus 11; Deuteronomy 14). We told her that there is nothing arbitrary about the matter. It is just that pork is filthy and unclean. And the Lord tells us that we will be much better off if we do not use it. In a cubic inch of pork there are as

124

many as forty thousand trichina worms. And we covered briefly the whole question of clean and unclean meats. Scavengers are not to be eaten, and so on.

Then I said, "Now not *all* our church members are vegetarians."

"Oh," she said, "I am."

"*You* are!" I exclaimed.

"Yes," she assured me, "I am."

"You are! When did *you* become a vegetarian?" I asked eagerly.

"Why," she said, "the night you preached on it."

"When did I preach on it?" I asked. "I don't remember preaching on that subject at any time in *this* place."

"Why," she replied, "don't you remember when you talked to that little class about it?"

I tried to think what she meant. All I had said in the class was, "I have the right to tell the world why I am a vegetarian, but I have no right to condemn anybody else for eating meat." And I added, "I am a vegetarian because flesh is so diseased. And I have a right to tell people how much healthier I feel being a vegetarian. The animal kingdom is so diseased today that I cannot, under ordinary circumstances, trust taking any of it into my system." And that was all I said about the matter.

But the woman went on to explain, "When you preached on it that night, I said to myself, 'Well, if vegetarianism is good for Brother Coon, it is good for me.' So I haven't touched meat since."

And I thought to myself, "Can you imagine that! This woman becomes a vegetarian on the basis of my personal testimony!"

I want to be a true witness for Jesus, don't you? Yes, indeed, just a witness. I tell our people—and our preachers too—that if I am eating beside a preacher who eats meat, bless your heart, that does not make a bit of difference to me. I think, "Maybe his stomach requires it." Who am I to judge his stomach? I am not a physician! You and I should be able to sit at a table where anyone can eat anything he needs to, and not have even one thought of criticism toward him. I have my hands full watching my own life, to make sure that I am ready to meet Jesus myself. What about you? And so all the Lord asks of me is to be a witness. "Ye are my witnesses, saith the Lord" (Isa. 43:10, 12).

The burden of judging, and denouncing, and condemning is very heavy, but it is a joy and a pleasure to witness for Jesus.

TWINS

"How would you suggest we work to win our husbands?" began a pair of twins in a revival afterservice recently. Then one of them related their experience.

One of the women had brought the truths of the Word of God to her sister. But in doing so, she had condemned her brother-in-law. Now they were not even on speaking terms. And besides that, her own husband was greatly prejudiced also. Being in town on business, she had come to the meeting that night. But since she lived at some distance, she remarked that it would be impossible for her to return again. She was sure her prejudiced husband would never allow her to have the car and make that long trip again.

"Why don't you both go home and just love your husbands?" I suggested. "Do not argue with them, do not even talk back in any heated discussion," I continued.

"Do you think I should apologize to my sister's husband, since we are not on speaking terms?" questioned the twin living at the greater distance.

"I believe the Holy Spirit is impressing you to, and I

126

believe I would," I replied. "And then return tomorrow night, if possible, and report the outcome of your being especially nice to your husbands."

"Oh, I shall never be able to be back during this series of meetings," exclaimed the twin from the far city. "You don't know my husband. He is terribly prejudiced against my church."

"Well, you never can tell what may happen under this new plan," I suggested. And with that they both thanked me for my suggestions and returned to their homes.

Two nights later both women were back at the service, as happy as could be. The one sang a solo and the other accompanied her at the piano. I could see from every expression on their faces that they had something good to report, even in this short period of time.

And sure enough, at the close of the service they were both in the prayer room for the afterservice. They could scarcely wait to give their experiences, especially the one who had not been on speaking terms with her brother-in-law, and whose husband was so terribly prejudiced.

"I went home," she began, "and tried to put into practice what you had suggested about not talking back, not condemning, or judging. And what do you suppose happened about noon today?"

"I don't know. Tell me," I replied, eager to learn the outcome.

"Well, my husband came in and said, 'Are those meetings still on?'

" 'Yes,' I said.

" 'Do you want to go again tonight?' Of course I told him I would love to go. And with that he pulled out a five-dollar bill and handed it to me."

In the excitement of their story—for they were both bubbling over with joy—I did not get the word-for-word

127

account of just what happened next. But in effect, he told her, "Take that [the five-dollar bill], fill up the tank with gas, and go back to the meetings and get some more of what you got the other night."

Not *all* in this old world are too hard to appreciate true Christianity when they see it demonstrated. Let us, therefore, cease to be judges or prosecuting attorneys. Let us only be witnesses of the wonderful gospel of Christ, showing its power to make and keep us loving, kind, and wholesome Christians. And who knows but that we may win those we thought would never accept Christ!

Jesus Inspires Hope

~~~~~~

*L*UCY WAS planning to marry out of Christ. I
was calling on her with her pastor. We were
trying to persuade her not to make the mistake
of marrying one who is not a Christian. As we were talking
with Lucy I was thinking to myself, "One of the outstanding principles of soul winning is to recognize that everyone must make his own choice. I cannot *force* anyone's
decision. Therefore, I cannot exert pressure on Lucy not to
marry this young man. But maybe I can build up in her a
hope, a confidence, a realization of what she may become
if she does not marry out of Christ. For the Scriptures declare that 'we are saved by hope' (Rom. 8:24)."

As Lucy and her pastor were chatting together I was
silently asking my Lord to help me to know the very words
I should say to her. Finally I looked up and began: "Lucy,
do you know what I think? I think there are infinite possibilities for you. I would not be surprised to see you a
nurse or a foreign missionary someday."

She looked at me in astonishment. "I mean that," I
affirmed.

Did I have a right to make such a statement? Surely I
did! There *are* infinite possibilities in every soul, aren't

there? We ought to know *that* after we have learned what is wrapped up in *one* atom. So I repeated, "There are just *infinite* possibilities in you, Lucy." And she really was a very fine young woman.

After a little reflection she replied, "Brother Coon, do you know, I have felt several times that God *could* use me to be a foreign missionary."

Her Lord, you see, had been impressing her with her possibilities. But the evil one was suggesting, "It's *not* for you. *You* could never be a worker for Christ." So she was having a real mental conflict.

HER MARRIED SISTER

As we chatted together Lucy's older sister, Grace, who lived about five miles away, dropped in. Grace had been married about five years. We had not talked long before Grace interrupted the conversation with, "That sister of mine! I have been trying to knock some sense into her head. But I can't."

The sister spoke wiser than she knew. Too many of us have been trying to *knock* things into people's heads. And that type of counseling just does not succeed.

"I made a fool of myself," Grace continued sadly, "and now my sister is going to do the same. She won't listen to anything I say. She is still going right ahead and marry that young man who is not a Christian."

Then warming up still more she said, "Five years ago someone told me I would be doing wrong if I married out of Christ. But I would not listen. I married just the same. Now see where I am!"

When I found a place where I could break in without appearing to be ungracious, I turned to Grace and said, "Do you know what I think? I think the Lord sent you here."

She felt complimented. I imagine she thought I meant the Lord had sent her there to scold her sister. But I did not mean that. I meant that I thought the Lord had sent her there so we could help *her*. However, I did not say that.

After a while Grace again blurted out, "That is just what I have been telling my sister. But you can't knock anything into her head!"

And I thought to myself, "Then why don't you stop trying? Why not use some other method?" But of course I did not put that thought into words.

So I turned to Grace again and repeated my former assertion, "I believe the Lord sent you here." She smiled again, and seemed to appreciate the comment very much. Finally, after several interruptions from Grace, I turned to her with, "You know, I wouldn't be surprised if *today* were your decision day." She smiled, and I thought she was just about ready to give her heart to Christ right then.

No Hope

The conversation continued a little longer. Then turning to Grace, I suggested: "Maybe you *do* want to decide for Christ today."

Her expression quickly changed from a smile to one of sadness as she replied, "Brother Coon, there is *no hope* for me."

"What do you mean?" I questioned.

"Well," she said, "when I was thinking of marrying out of Christ, about five years ago, a Christian worker came to see me. He told me that if I did, I would probably be committing the unpardonable sin." Then she added sorrowfully, "So you see, there has been no hope for me all these years."

"Why, Grace," I began warmly and assuringly, "if you still have a desire to serve God, that means you are still

131

hearing His voice. And if you are hearing His voice, and there is a desire on your part to serve Him, you have not committed the unpardonable sin. Do you still have a desire to serve the Lord?"

"Yes, I do," she replied.

"Then *you* have not committed the unpardonable sin," I smiled confidently.

We talked on together a little more. Then her eyes brightened as she said meditatively, "It is really true that a *few* times during the last five years it seems I have almost had a little ray of hope." She was beginning to find her way back to God. It was because the Lord had used us to inspire her with "hope." "For we are saved by hope" (Rom. 8:24).

Why was it that Grace had been conscious at times that there might be a possibility of hope for her? Ah, the Lord was keeping alive the spark of hope in her heart. But no member of the church had encouraged her or suggested to her that there still was hope. God's plan is for Christians to go to the side of a discouraged soul and bring him hope in Jesus, "for we are saved by hope" (Rom. 8:24).

"THERE IS NO HOPE FOR ME"

Grace's is not an isolated case. Such experiences are taking place all around us. I recall the experience of another young woman. Her pastor and I had visited her together. On the way to her home the pastor had mentioned the word "disfellowshipment."

"Oh," I said, "she does not need disfellowshipment. All she needs is for us to bring her hope. 'For we are saved by hope.'" I did not then know that two weeks before, upon her own request, her name had been stricken from the church records.

As we conversed with this young woman in her home,

I said, "Sister, I have something for you. I *know* you can be saved." Her face lighted up as we continued our conversation.

The next day, I think it was, she wrote a letter to her pastor. In it she remarked, "Pastor, it was so good of you ministers to come and visit me. Of course there is no hope for me now. But if there had been, you certainly would have brought it to me that morning."

What a sad condition! If she could have received two or three more such visits from the Christians of her church, she doubtless would have been inspired with hope to begin all over again. I hope the pastor directed them to follow our lead. "For we are saved by hope" (Rom. 8:24).

It is not too difficult for any of us to go to the side of one whom the devil has discouraged, and say, "Brother (Sister), 'though your sins be as scarlet, they shall be as white as snow' (Isa. 1:18). Let me help you place your hand in the nail-scarred hand of Jesus. The promise is, 'Him that cometh to me I will in no wise cast out'" (John 6:37). If even a *few* members would step to the side of a discouraged one with such words of faith and hope, he probably would never request the church to take his name from the records. It is just that simple. "For we are saved by hope" (Rom. 8:24). May God forgive us for our thoughtlessness and neglect! May He help us to keep our eyes open to aid some struggling soul who is in need of *hope*. Let us point him to Jesus the Saviour of the world.

"Saved by Hope"

In this section we are studying the topic, "Saved by Hope." We want to learn how we can all do our little part to help people to be saved in God's eternal kingdom. We want to stop trying to "knock something" into their heads. Many people seem to think the science of soul winning is too complicated for them. It *is* a deep science, to be sure. But its principles are simple. It *can* be understood. But what saith the Scriptures? "Say not in thine heart, Who shall ascend into heaven? (that is, to bring Christ down from above:) or, Who shall descend into the deep? (that is, to bring up Christ again from the dead.) But what saith it? The word is nigh thee" (Rom. 10:6-9). The principle is very simple: "For we are saved by hope" (Rom. 8:24).

We are so accustomed to quoting the scripture that declares, "By grace are ye saved through faith" (Eph. 2: 8), that we may forget there is anything else that enters into the picture that is fully as simple. The text we are studying here declares, "We are saved by hope." *Hope* is the combination, or the result, of grace and faith.

Hope is a wonderful thing. It is *so* wonderful that we are *saved* by it. Did you know that it is for this reason the Bible was given? "That we through patience and comfort of the scriptures might have hope" (Rom. 15:4). Yes, indeed, that is the purpose for which the Scriptures were given. The object of every Bible study, of every sermon, of every missionary visit should be to inspire the struggling soul with—what? HOPE. And Jesus Christ is our hope.

CHRIST—SINNER—SATAN

Now, Jesus knows that sinners are "saved by hope." And Satan is aware of the same fact. So since Christ knows that sinners are "saved by hope," what will He do? "The Lord is keeping alive the spark of hope in their hearts."— *Testimonies to Ministers,* p. 354.

But Satan, over on the other side of the sinner, also knows that sinners are "saved by hope." So what does *he* desire to do? "Satan . . . desires to take every glimmer of hope and every ray of light from the soul."—*Steps to Christ,* p. 53 (pocket ed.).

134

So a battle follows. Satan struggles to take every glimmer of hope from the soul, while Jesus patiently fans the spark to keep it alive. It is a battle of HOPE. Christ is continually keeping alive the spark of hope in his heart. Satan is constantly trying to take away the last ray of hope. Satan says, "You have gone too far. There is no use of your trying any more. You've taken a step in the wrong direction. You might just as well take another." Thus Satan seeks to lead the sinner farther and farther into sin and despair. He continues, "Don't you see? You are just a hypocrite anyway? You are *so* weak. You are unworthy. Salvation is not for you."

What is Satan trying to do through such suggestions? He is trying to discourage, to take every glimmer of hope from the soul.

And while the poor sinner is listening, wavering, not knowing what to answer, the Lord Jesus speaks in a still small voice, "Come unto me, all ye that labour and are heavy laden, and I will give you rest" (Matt. 11:28). "Look unto me, and be ye saved" (Isa. 45:22). Thus "the Lord is keeping alive the spark of hope in their hearts."—*Testimonies to Ministers,* p. 354.

WHERE WE COME IN

About that time I, as a Christian worker, come into the picture. I begin to denounce this sinner. I say, "My, but you have made a mess of things! You have brought disgrace on your wife. You have brought reproach on your family!" On whose side am I? On Satan's side, of course. And he has his arm, as it were, right around me, for we are partners in dispensing discouragement. And the devil is doubtless rejoicing. I am playing right into his hands, because Satan for many years may have whispered those same words into the sinner's ears. And now he has a helper in the person of a *minister of the gospel!* And I may return home and report that I made a missionary visit. Can you imagine that? One missionary visit for whom?—the devil.

Then I go to my friends and say, "I tell you, I gave *him* something to think about. I told him off all right." All the time I am thinking I have accomplished some great feat. But Satan flies back to the other demons and reports with hellish glee, "We certainly are going to have that man. Coon made a missionary visit to him for *us* today!"

But instead of that, suppose I come into the picture differently. I realize I am the weakest layman in the church. I feel I cannot successfully conduct a Bible study or do much of anything else to help. But I see this poor sinner. My heart is touched. My soul reaches out to him in love. I go to his side, and with trembling voice and tear-dimmed eyes, say, "Brother, there is still hope for you."

By speaking just that one simple sentence, on whose side am I? I am on Christ's side, because Christ is fanning that little spark of HOPE. And if I also fan it, and if there are a number of other Christians who will do the same, before we know it that man may be "saved by hope." The spark has become a flame, by a few timid, perhaps, but loving Christians joining together with Christ to keep alive the spark of hope before it dies out.

JESUS' WAY

Everywhere Jesus went "He sought to inspire with hope the most rough and unpromising, setting before them the assurance that they might become blameless and harmless, attaining such a character as would make them manifest as the children of God. Often He met those who had drifted under Satan's control, and who had no power to break from his snare. To such a one, discouraged, sick, tempted, and fallen, Jesus would speak words of tenderest pity, words that were needed and could be understood. Others He met who were fighting a hand-to-hand battle with the adversary of souls. These He encouraged to persevere, assuring them that they would win; for angels of God were on their side, and would give them the victory. Those whom He thus helped were convinced that here was One in whom they could trust with perfect confidence. He would not betray the secrets they poured into His sympathizing ear."—*The Desire of Ages,* pp. 91, 92.

The Word of God declares that "hope maketh not ashamed" (Rom. 5:5). "For thou art my hope, O Lord God" (Ps. 71:5). God does not embarrass the repentant sinner. Neither should we. We are to teach the sinner, the wayward, to "look up" (Luke 21:28). The promises of God's Word and the attitude of Christ toward the sinner, bring hope "which hope we have as an anchor of the soul, both sure and stedfast" (Heb. 6:19).

A Backslider

Several years ago there was a man in our church who had left his wife and children. He had gone to a nearby city and rented an apartment. This was about nine miles from where my wife and I happened to be living at the time.

One of the leading officers in the church came to me one day exclaiming, "Brother Coon, there is Brother Blank. You know, *that* man must be dealt with at once." The inference was strong. It was a suggestion that he must be disciplined, perhaps disfellowshiped, at once.

"Do you know where he is living now?" I inquired. And the church officer informed me where the man was staying in the city.

"I will call him on the telephone and make an appointment with him, and see if I can help him," I remarked.

137

"Call him on the telephone! Why, I should say not! If you ever call that man on the telephone, and he knows that you want to talk with him, you will *never* get to see him. The only way to get to see *that* man is to come on him suddenly, and, as it were, beard the lion in his den," was his reply.

But I took a Bible promise. It was, "If any of you lack wisdom, let him ask of God" (James 1:5-8). Then I claimed another Bible promise for this backslidden brother: "If any man see his brother sin a sin which is not unto death, he shall ask, and he shall give him life" (1 John 5:16).

Then prayerfully claiming these two promises, I called Mr. Blank on the telephone. I began enthusiastically, "Brother Blank, I am your new pastor. I have some *wonderful* news for you! Something you will like very much. But I must see you all alone. And I would like to see you after dark, so no one will know anything about it. I would like to meet you in my car, in my driveway, so we can be entirely alone. It is confidential."

"I'll be there tonight," he replied quickly. Friends, in just a few seconds it was all done. The appointment was made—that appointment the church officer thought utterly impossible.

With what had the Lord helped me to already inspire this backslider?—with HOPE! I had something wonderful for him. It was also confidential.

IN MY CAR

At the appointed moment Mr. Blank was at my home. It was dark. Quietly he stepped into the front seat of the car and sat down by my side.

"Brother," I immediately began, with all the enthusiasm

138

I could muster, and with a prayer in my heart, "I have something wonderful for you, just as I told you on the telephone. It is nothing financial, but I have come to bring you victory over sin."

It seemed as though I could see him slump in the seat at that expression, "victory over sin." And I saw right then that he was not even going to look at me. During the next thirty or forty minutes, only occasionally did he look my way. And then it was a look from the corner of his eye, without turning his head. I felt I knew what he was thinking. He was probably wondering, "Is this preacher claiming to be my friend, but merely gathering information to use later against me?" And I could not exactly blame him, if that is what he was thinking. For some of us Christians may have been guilty of that approach.

So he sat there just staring straight ahead. Only his eyes were turned in my direction occasionally. To me that meant, "I don't know whether I dare to trust you or not. I wonder if you are trying to trap me." But he was not saying a word.

I continued kindly, and with a continual prayer in my heart, "Brother Blank, I have come to help you." And then I spent ten, fifteen, twenty minutes, assuring him of my true interest in him. I told him some of the confidential experiences I had had with other men. I added, "No one has ever known their names in connection with these problems." I mentioned men in the church who had been in a condition similar to his, and had come out victorious. I was trying to inspire him with hope. "Now some of them are ordained ministers," I continued hopefully. "They are now winning many souls to Christ," I assured him. And I pointed out, "If I had ever broken their confidence, instead of being soul winners today, they might be out in the world." What was I trying to do? I was trying to cooperate

139

with God and inspire him with HOPE. "For we are saved by hope" (Rom. 8:24).

But Mr. Blank only continued to stare into space. I felt I knew what that poor soul was thinking. Yes, he was doubtless thinking, "I wonder! I wonder if the preacher is trying to wring a confession from me. Then he may recommend that I be disfellowshiped from the church."

Satan tried to discourage me. When, after many, many minutes, there was no response, Satan suggested to me that there was no use of trying to help a man who did not even appreciate it. But I kept on talking confidentially, hopefully, kindly, for twenty minutes, for thirty minutes, for forty minutes! Yes, I continued for forty *long* minutes, assuring that poor soul that I was his friend. I told him that I was there to help him to be saved. I knew he could and *would* be saved.

All the while I was speaking, my heart was laying hold of the promise: "If any man see his brother sin a sin which is not unto death, he shall ask, and he [God] shall give him life for them that sin not unto death" (1 John 5:16).

After about forty minutes it finally dawned on Mr. Blank that I *really* was there to *help* him. I was truly his friend. And then all at once his head dropped into his hands and he began to sob like a child. "Brother Coon," he wept, "I don't believe there is any hope for me."

Ah, friends, who had been telling him that? Satan had. The devil had preached that to him for a long, long time. But there had not been *one person* in the church who had ever encouraged him during the terrific Gethsemane through which he was passing. Not one! There were those who could point the finger of scorn at him and say, "You are a hypocrite." *That* is what Satan had been doing for a long time. But I was doing only what any church member could do. I was fanning the little spark of hope in his heart. I was cooperating with Him who says, "We are saved by hope."

QUOTING HOPEFUL SCRIPTURES

As Mr. Blank continued to sob out his grief I put my arm around him and began to pat him gently on the shoulder. Then I quoted to him such hopeful texts of Scripture as, "If we confess our sins, he is faithful and just to forgive us our sins, and to cleanse us from all unrighteousness" (1 John 1:9).

"Brother," I continued, "as surely as you are confessing your sins to God tonight, He is cleansing you. All the past is *in* the *past.* For, 'though your sins be as scarlet, they shall be as white as snow; though they be red like crimson, they shall be as wool' (Isa. 1:18). 'Him that cometh to me I will in no wise cast out' (John 6:37). 'Come unto me, all ye that labour and are heavy laden, and I will give you rest' (Matt. 11:28)." As I spoke, I found my heart warm with love, and my eyes filled with tears.

I added fervently, "Brother, you are now experiencing the new birth, as your heart is breaking before God. Jesus is bringing you victory *now.* You *are* His child. You are turning from the wicked way. You *are* turning to God. And He promises, 'A broken and a contrite heart, O God, thou wilt not despise' (Ps. 51:17). 'Thus saith the high and lofty One that inhabiteth eternity, whose name is Holy; I dwell in the high and holy place, with him also that is of a contrite and humble spirit, to revive the spirit of the humble, and to revive the heart of the contrite ones' (Isa. 57:15)."

Then I began to unfold to him the great work I believed he was going to do for his Lord. After several moments of this, suddenly he raised his head and looked me

141

full in the face. Oh, that meant something! I knew he had made a decision!

"Brother Coon," he exclaimed in brokenheartedness, "I'm going home."

Friends, I cannot tell you how those words, "I'm going home," thrilled me. "Praise the Lord!" I exclaimed. "When are you going? Tonight?"

"No," he replied, "I'm going tomorrow."

"Wonderful," I answered. I knew then that I could get over to his home first and prepare his wife to welcome him.

As I bade him good night I retired with a prayer of thanksgiving to Him who declares we are "saved by hope."

VISITING HIS WIFE

The next morning I hastened over to the home to see his wife, that I might bring *her* hope too. As I walked in I began just as enthusiastically as possible, "Sister Blank, your husband was converted last night, and he is coming home. And he is going to serve the Lord."

But what a disappointment awaited me. She looked at me as though she could eat and digest nails!

"Hm-hm-hm! Oh, yes! He needs to be converted! Hm-hm! He needs to be converted!" she sneered. "You think he is? You think *he* is! Hm!"

"Yes, Sister Blank," I replied with all the fervor I could display, "God came in last night in a wonderful way, and the Holy Spirit melted your husband's heart."

"Hm-hm! Better melt it! Better melt it!" she sneered again.

In talking with her husband the night before, when much time had passed, the devil said, "Don't fuss with that man any more." The devil wanted me to give up hope. But I did not heed his suggestion. And God helped me to go through with the ordeal, and gave victory. But now, this morning, as his wife was talking, I listened to the devil. Really, as I looked into that woman's face I listened to Satan. I thought, "Anybody but a Pharisee! What *can* you do for a self-satisfied religionist?"

I always believed that God had given me my wife. I have always known that, because I prayed for her, and God answered my prayer. But my wife, in all of our married life, had never seemed so precious to me as she did when I looked into Mrs. Blank's face that memorable morning. And right there I thanked God all over again for my wife. I was saying in my heart, "Thank God I don't have to live with *that* woman!" Really I was!

Then the devil spoke in full force to me: "Coon, go home. You can't do anything with that woman. Anything but a Pharisee! A brokenhearted sinner is easy to reclaim in comparison with a self-righteous, self-satisfied, professed Christian," he whispered strongly and convincingly.

And friends, for a moment I believed what Satan said. It was so truthful, even though the devil was saying it. But the Lord came to my rescue again. He said, "I helped you last night with her husband. Maybe this woman has had a pretty difficult time with him after all." Then I could hear the Lord speaking to my heart something like this: "Coon, if you will express confidence in her as you did in her husband last night, she will be saved by hope also." And then I prayed earnestly that God would help me to inspire *her* with hope, even though it did seem impossible. But how *could* I speak faith under such discouraging circumstances?

In answer to my prayer, God helped me to say something I myself had to take purely by faith. "Sister Blank," I began smilingly, "do you know what you are going to do when your husband comes home? I am making a prediction. My prediction is that when your husband comes you

143

will rush out on the front porch. You will throw your arms around him. You will give him the warmest welcome of his life. He needs it, and it will mean his salvation."

And then came her reply. It came to me as a shock. "That's *just* what I am going to do." And when she said that I thought I was going to faint—almost! I could scarcely believe such a wonderful change could take place in so short a time. But now she had hope, you see. God had helped me to inspire her with HOPE.

We knelt down and prayed. There on my knees in the front room of that home I thanked God for her kindness and love. I praised the Lord that she was willing to take her husband back. Then I bade her good day and went on my way—faint, but victorious. The battle of HOPE had been a terrific struggle of faith and love.

"DADDY IS BACK HOME"

A few days later I was in a nearby grocery store. Their little boy came in while I was back among the shelves. There were not many people in the store. So I edged around to where the little fellow was, so he and I could be more or less alone. Then I spoke to him in a subdued tone. "Son," I said, "how is everything at your home?" And I waited eagerly for the reply.

I think I shall never forget how he reacted to that question. He was just a little fellow. But he straightened up with such assurance, and his face was beaming. He looked into my eyes as much as to say, "Now, you know all about what I am saying." And then he exclaimed quietly, "Fine!" Hesitating a bit, he continued very confidentially, "Daddy is back home."

"Daddy is back home!" What a reward for the terrible struggle with the two parents. "Daddy is back home!" Oh, how much that expression contained! Friends, I want to

144

tell you, my heart felt so warm. All inside, I was crying in thankfulness to God that He had saved Mr. Blank by hope. It had been a terrific struggle. Satan tried to cause me to give up because of the apparent hardness of heart. But God had helped me to persevere until both parents were "saved by hope."

There are souls today out in the night of sin, far from home. They long for home and happiness. They crave release from bondage. They pray for restoration and salvation. The devil has caused them to fear that their condition is hopeless. They are despairing under the cruel suggestions of the enemy of their souls. *Isa 47:10 + 1Jn 4:18*

But "the Lord is keeping alive the spark of hope in their hearts."—*Testimonies to Ministers*, p. 354. His Spirit calls for human helpers—helpers who will fly to their side and not become discouraged because they appear careless or hard, difficult or uncourteous. The Lord wants you, my brother, my sister, to go to them in confidence, not upholding them in sin, but kindly, prayerfully, lovingly showing them the way back to their Father's house.

When earth's little season of sin is finished, Jesus wants many a boy and girl to be able to cry out in gleefulness, "Daddy is back home!" To see the smiles of eternal bliss on the faces of those for whom we have prayed, and with whom we have wept, and for whom we have struggled, will be reward enough to all who have been willing to see behind the rough exterior of an apparently careless soul, and help him to be "saved by hope."

CARELESS

A young woman came to me one day. She related to me an experience I hope never to forget. She was considered most careless by her teachers and associates at the college of which church I happened to be serving as pastor. But as

10

she talked with me I learned that she spent hours at a time sobbing out her remorse to God. It was in her room alone. No one knew. No one heard—except God. Flinging herself on her bed, she had wept for hours at a time, while the voice of the evil one whispered that there was no hope for her.

Oh, how happy I was that it had been my privilege to look beyond the mask of carelessness and see possibilities in one who may be "saved by hope."

Do you say, "I cannot give Bible studies"? Are you thinking, "I cannot preach, or pray publicly, or even give talks as some others do"? Friends, there is one thing you *can* do. You can move quietly, confidentially, to the side of a depressed, discouraged heart, and whisper HOPE. You can quote the wonderful promises of infinite love. You can look beyond the rough exterior to the sincerity of a human heart. By faith you can reach out and supplicate the throne of grace for the erring, the wandering, the lost, and the sinful.

Then, someday, in the eternal kingdom of our wonderful Lord, the words will be uttered, "Back home!" Yes, "Back home," in a heaven where sorrows can nevermore come. "Back home," in a place where there will be no disappointments. "Back home," where all will be light, happiness, joy, and peace. O what a reward to those who have cooperated with our precious Saviour in saving blood-bought souls from death by His wonderful, wonderful love!

PICTURE OF HOPE

Some time ago there hung in the Tate Gallery of London a painting by Watts. A beautiful young woman is pictured as blindfolded. In her hand is a stringed instrument called a lute. But every string is broken, except one. With an in-

146

tense expression of earnestness on her face, her hand draws the bow over the one remaining string—taut, but not yet broken. And underneath the picture is just one word, "Hope."

The world today has tried almost every known string, hoping to produce harmony in place of discord. It has sought long and hard to find peace instead of war, prosperity in place of depression, and happiness in place of sorrow.

Discouraged, wandering souls are in their world of darkness. Their day has turned to night. Their lives are confused and defeated. They are vainly struggling to make a melody from frustrated lives. The last string seems about to snap. They are coming to the end of their efforts. Satan whispers to their discouraged souls, "It is too late. You are lost. There is no use of trying any more." But "the Lord is keeping alive the spark of hope in their hearts."

And now His sweet voice whispers tenderly to you, "Take my yoke upon you, and learn of me; for I am meek and lowly in heart: and ye shall find rest unto your souls" (Matt. 11:29).

Will you become a partner of the wonderful Jesus? Will you take the priceless principle of "hope" to those who are waiting for someone to balance their decision toward eternal life? Oh, it will make you so happy to see precious souls saved, eternally saved, in God's wonderful heaven, because you and I have cooperated with Him who declares, "we are saved by hope."

Jesus Quickens Faith

~~~~~~

A LITTLE BOY went to Sabbath school and was placed beside a little girl. In fright he began crying. But in time he overcame his timidity. At the age of twelve he looked across the schoolroom and saw a redheaded girl. He thought she was the most beautiful human being he had ever beheld! He did not know then that girls are like buses—if you miss the first one, another will be along in a few minutes.

The redheaded girl and he did not make a go of it for very long. He again looked across the schoolroom and saw another girl, Louisa. And right then he thought that although Louisa did not have red hair, nevertheless she was truly the most lovely person he had ever seen.

In sheer delight he fell in love with her, then and there. So they began a friendship. Then the little boy and the little girl began to write notes to each other during school or recess. But when the boy opened his arithmetic book he saw "two times two equals—Louisa." And when he opened his geography book, all he could see in his imagination was the map of Louisa. When he looked into his grammar book the words that appealed to him seemed to be "dear" and "sweetheart"—Louisa!

He was beginning to understand that girls and studies do not mix. But it was difficult by then to get his eyes and heart off of Louisa. He was a little captive to infatuation. He and his brother went down to the local post office and talked with the postmistress. "Would you kindly keep the mail that comes for us," they began, "and not give it to anyone else?"

The postmistress drew the little boys out a bit. "Do you mean not to give your mail to your parents?"

The boys cleared their throats a bit and hardly knew what to say. They finally, hesitatingly, let the postmistress know that was about what they had in mind.

"Oh, I couldn't hold your mail back from your parents," she made very clear to the boys.

Quickly they let her know that that was not "exactly" what they had in mind. But it really was. They just became frightened for fear she would tell their parents on them. And of course that would result in their getting a good whipping.

About that time the younger of the two boys overheard mother confiding in father, "I am worried over Jimmy. He is writing notes to the girls. But Glenn—he would *never* do that. I have all the confidence in the world in Glenn."

Glenn was listening, and heard those magic words of faith. And do you know what that faith expressed in Glenn did for him? It caused him to make a resolution, and that was that he would never write any more notes to the girls while he was in grammar school.

And he didn't either. What was it that gave him the power to break with Louisa? It was the faith his mother had expressed in him. Of course his mother did not know that he was so wrapped up in love! But her expressed confidence was rewarded.

"And this is the victory that overcometh the world, even our faith" (1 John 5:4). Next to love, faith is probably the most powerful principle in the universe. We should therefore use it in our words, in our actions, and in our lives continually if we would win souls from the paths of darkness into the light of Jesus Christ.

THE DISCIPLES

Let us see in what kind of men Jesus expressed faith. How many apostles did He first choose? Twelve. And one of those men was "a devil" (John 6:70). So one twelfth of the early church was a devil. What would you think if one twelfth of your local membership were devils? We would think that would ruin the whole church. But that is only the beginning. Let us look a little farther.

Another one of Christ's first followers was a doubter (John 20:24, 25). He was doubting Thomas. And that takes care of one sixth of His church membership. So one was a devil, and another was a doubter. And the one is just about as bad as the other.

Then there was another who stood and warmed himself by the fire during Christ's trial. When someone accosted him, saying, "Art not thou also one of this man's disciples?" he denied Him and said, "I am not" (John 18:17). He was a denier. That was Simon Peter. So that takes care of three twelfths, or a quarter of the whole group. One twelfth a devil, one twelfth a doubter, and one twelfth a denier!

And then two others were "sons of thunder" (Mark 3:17).

That takes care of one, two, three, four, five—five twelfths, almost half of them already.

And what about the other seven twelfths? Often every last one of them got into a quarrel over who was going to

150

be the greatest (Mark 9:33, 34). Now, wasn't that some Christian group for Jesus to try to do anything with?

CHRIST EXPRESSED FAITH

But what kind of confidence did Jesus express in that group? He said to one of them, "I have prayed for thee, that thy faith fail not: and when thou art converted, strengthen thy brethren" (Luke 22:32). In other words, Jesus was saying to Peter, "Peter, you are going to be converted. Then you will strengthen your brethren." And to all of them, with the exception of Judas, He said, "Ye shall receive power, after that the Holy Ghost is come upon you: and ye shall be witnesses unto me" (Acts 1:8).

What wonderful faith to express in that kind of individuals! Isn't it marvelous? Think of Jesus saying to *them,* "Go ye therefore, and teach all nations, baptizing them" (Matt. 28:19). Do you mean that a man who would curse and swear, as did Peter, was to go out and baptize others into Jesus Christ? Do you say that a man who was a doubter, like Thomas, was to teach and immerse people in the name of Jesus? Are you telling us that men who were thunderous, like James and John, were to preach and baptize? Yes, indeed! And not merely that, but Jesus also added the assuring promise, "Lo, I am with you alway, even unto the end of the world" (Matt. 28:20).

You know, it is simply wonderful, the faith and confidence that Jesus expressed in those poor, erring men, and in what they would become through His Holy Spirit. But Jesus went farther than that. He promised them that whatever they bound on earth—so long as they would abide by certain simple rules—would be bound in heaven. What authority! What faith! What confidence in a sinful group of men!

151

BELIEVE IN ONE ANOTHER

If Christ, the sinless One, had such confidence in that group of erring men, should we not have confidence in one another? Yes, indeed. We should believe every man is sincere at heart.

If we would see a man gain the victory over any besetment, what is the *best* way to help him? Express *faith* in him. Jesus did that. When Nathanael first came to Jesus he was prejudiced. But Jesus exclaimed as He saw him coming, "Behold an Israelite indeed, in whom is no guile" (John 1:47-49).

Was Nathanael a member of Christ's church at that time? No! Then is it right and proper for me, an Adventist, to say of a Methodist who loves the Lord and is living up to the light he understands, "Behold an Israelite indeed?" Yes, of course it is. The same would be true of any Christian believer. That is the way to help and encourage people. Let us also express confidence in those who are not now Christians. Let us suggest what they may become by accepting the Lord Jesus Christ.

In order to freely express confidence in others I must believe that others are sincere. I would prefer to believe everyone is sincere and be let down by some than to misjudge even one truly sincere person, wouldn't you? Can a wicked man be sincere in his wickedness? Of course he can. The apostle Paul declared that he was most sincere in his persecution of Christ in the person of His followers. The Scriptures declare that Eve, who brought the first sin into the world, was deceived. The book of Revelation declares that the world will be deceived. Therefore we are to look into everyone's face and think, "That person is sincere." He may indeed be deceived, but he may be ever so honest at heart. Therefore my responsibility under God is not to denounce him, but to enlighten him; not to condemn him, but to find the path to his heart. I can do this by expressions of faith and confidence in him. Then only can I hope to enlighten a heart that is darkened.

HOW TO EXPRESS FAITH

If we would help others toward the kingdom, let us express *faith* in them as Jesus did. Suppose a husband has an unbelieving wife. In introducing her to a minister he says, "Pastor Blank, this is my wife. She is a little stubborn." Would that help his wife to become a Christian? Would that incline her heart to love Jesus? Why, no, of course not.

Would not this be a better method? "Pastor Blank, meet my wife. She does not happen to be a member of *my* church. But I want to tell you, she is a darling!"

The preacher might greet her warmly and say, "That is fine. She looks like a very kindhearted woman."

The wife would more than likely be thinking, "I believe I would enjoy being a Christian if that is the way they act. They are a *kind* people." Now, isn't that about the way it would work?

How about our children? Should we ever look at one of them and exclaim to someone else, "That boy is stubborn. He just does not want to do what is right." No! No! We should never, never suggest anything of the kind. Our confidence in them brings victory. I have no right even to suggest that a loved one or a neighbor is stubborn. The moment I mention that, I am making myself a judge. But I *do* have a right to allow that my friend is honest. I have a perfect right to do that. I am not judging then. I am merely doing as Jesus did. He said, "Behold an Israelite indeed, in whom is no guile" (John 1:47-49).

153

You may recall that Nathanael, of whom Jesus is speaking here, was *very* prejudiced toward Jesus. But now when Jesus expressed faith in him, Nathanael opened his heart and said, "Rabbi, thou art the Son of God; thou art the King of Israel" (John 1:47-49). Do you see how fast the principle of faith worked?

CHRIST AND ZACCHAEUS

Walking along with the multitude one day, Jesus looked up into a tree and saw Zacchaeus sitting there (Luke 19:1-10). Zacchaeus, a rich man and a chief publican, had heard much of Jesus, and longed to see Him. When he heard Jesus was coming that way, being short of stature, he climbed a sycamore tree so as not to miss the opportunity of seeing Jesus.

Zacchaeus means "the pure one." Without a doubt, when he was born his mother hoped that he would be the deliverer of Israel. That was the fond hope of every Israelitish mother. So she called him "Zacchaeus," "the pure one." But as he grew up he was a disappointment. Whenever he heard that name it probably sounded to him like ridicule. It was as though people were making fun of him, "So *you* are the *pure* one, are you? Aha! Aha!"

As Jesus raised His eyes into the branches of that tree He looked right into the face of Zacchaeus. And the way Jesus so tenderly spoke his name, "Zacchaeus," thrilled that poor sinner and caused him to believe that he *could* be, if not *the* "pure one," at least *a* "pure one" again. Confidence was in the eyes and in the voice of the Master as He spoke kindly to a victim of sin. And more than that Jesus said, "Make haste, and come down; for today I must abide at thy house." And Zacchaeus scrambled down out of that tree and returned home, leading the large procession that followed Jesus.

154

When Jesus called to Zacchaeus and said, "I must abide at thy house," the record says that every person in that group murmured. That must have included the twelve disciples. They were doubtless thinking, "This is no way to deal with sinners. What an abominable, filthy thief is Zacchaeus! Is Jesus going to *his* home? Is He going to be a guest at *his* house? If Jesus only knew what kind of fellow he is, He would never do that!"

But Jesus said, "I am going to abide with you today, Zacchaeus." That is one of the ways Christ honored sinners, by coming under their roof and eating with them.

Zacchaeus said to Jesus in the hearing of the multitude, "I am going to give half of my goods to the poor. And I am going to pay back fourfold everybody I have robbed."

As Jesus was sitting in the home of Zacchaeus, He said with confidence in the hearing of the disciples, "This day is salvation come to this house."

Did Jesus' faith in Zacchaeus pay off? It surely did. Faith always pays dividends. Jesus found it so in His experience, over and over again. You and I will find it so if we will but try it. Yes, faith really pays. Expressed faith brings a real reward in souls saved—eternally saved!

Our *prayers* should also be full of faith. "Jesus sees His true church on the earth, whose greatest ambition is to cooperate with Him in the grand work of saving souls. He hears their prayers, presented in contrition and power, and Omnipotence can not resist their plea for the salvation of any tried, tempted member of Christ's body."—*Testimonies to Ministers*, pp. 19, 20.

DOUBT AND SIN

"Brother Coon," began a fine woman, "meet my husband and son." And I shook hands with two of the finest

155

appearing gentlemen any man could hope to greet. Neither of them was a member of the church.

In my heart I was just about ready to congratulate that fine woman for bringing these men to the revival meeting, when she spoke up again: "I can't get them to come to the meetings with me, Brother Coon."

That was the first time these men had ever set foot in our church, so far as I know. And doubtless it was the last. Why? Because this well-meaning woman had sinned by expressing doubt. "Whatsoever is not of faith is sin" (Rom. 14:23). "Without faith it is impossible to please him" (Heb. 11:6). For "this is the victory that overcometh the world, even our faith" (1 John 5:4).

We should never make the mistake this good woman did of giving voice to expressions that savor of doubt. That is a denial of the power of the gospel. It is also an infringement on the golden rule. Would *you* go to a church the second time with a friend of yours if the very first time you went he belittled you and expressed doubt in you before the minister? More than likely you would not. You might attend a funeral, or even a wedding, in that church, but it would have to be a very special occasion for you even to think of returning after such a remark of doubt had been expressed about you.

JIMMY WHITE

A pastor and I went to visit Jimmy White. His wife was a Christian. But Jimmy had a bad habit that irritated his wife, and probably hurt his Lord as well.

We had not been seated in Jimmy's house more than a few moments before Mrs. White began to make remarks about Jimmy's unfortunate habit. We were really there to help Jimmy overcome that habit. But the moment his wife expressed doubt in him before us, both *her* usefulness and *ours* was at an end, so far as Jimmy was concerned. She had embarrassed him. She had belittled him. She had expressed doubt in him. And the saddest part of it all was that she *thought* she was helping him. Had she later been asked if she had ever tried to help her husband to break with this enslaving habit of sin, she would without a doubt have referred to this very experience as evidence that she had done her best to aid him. But in actuality she had done about the worst thing a wife could do. It was practically impossible for us preachers to bring any help to Jimmy after that, for he associated us with his wife's words of doubt, criticism, and condemnation.

POOR MR. WRIGHT

"Isn't that a beautiful view over the city!" I exclaimed as we looked down over the bluff from the Wright home. (Now don't think I am using actual names. That would be unfair. I am using assumed names so as not to embarrass anyone whose friends might read this book.) As we gazed from the hilltop upon the glittering lights of the city below, Mrs. Wright, a very conscientious Christian, turned to me in the presence of her fine and noble-appearing husband, with the words, "Tell me, Pastor Coon, how can I get my husband to join my church? He does not want to do right."

I felt like sinking through the floor. There was that fine man standing right beside us. I put myself in his place, and I was terribly embarrassed for him. I was thinking to myself, "That has ended *her* usefulness so far as *he* is concerned."

I tried to turn the conversation to the beautiful city view. But again came the question: "Just what would *you* do if you were in *my* place? My husband is a fine man, but he is stubborn."

157

Friends, since I do not want to tell any wife before her non-Christian husband exactly what to do to help him to accept Christ, I am mentioning it here. It is this:

Express only faith in him. Do this when you are alone. Do it in company. Never, N-E-V-E-R, express a word of doubt. For "whatsoever is not of faith is sin" (Rom. 14:23). But in order to express faith in people, we must believe in people. I always, without exception, like to think of everyone I meet as being sincere at heart. Unless I take this attitude, all my expressions of faith are themselves insincere. Do you see?

LITTLE JOHNNIE

"My, you have a lovely son!" I exclaim to a mother. And little Johnnie stands there waiting for mother's reply. Mother's reply probably has more to do with Johnnie's future than most people suspect. If mother replies, "Johnnie is a goodhearted boy. He is full of life and energy and he is going to devote it all to the Lord," probably Johnnie will do just that. But if mother replies to my leading remark by saying, "Johnnie is always getting into trouble. He is a bad boy," then Johnnie will, without a doubt, grow up—other things being equal—to be just the boy mother pictures him to be.

If mother wants Johnnie to be a good boy, let her speak in his hearing only words of confidence. Expressed faith is a powerful aid in helping young people to make right decisions when passing through the crises of life.

The boy whom mother says is bad will in all probability decide that he *is* bad, and therefore is supposed to *act* bad. But the mother who explains that Johnnie is just full of energy will probably, with the wisdom God has offered, aid her boy in channeling his energies into useful pursuits. One need not lie. If a boy is bad, then

158

of course we should not say he is good. But we may still express faith that he will someday accept Jesus.

MR. AND MRS. AMES

A pastor and I visited Mr. and Mrs. Ames recently. They were people from Germany who had been in America but a short time. They spoke broken English. But they had studied the Bible, and were convinced that they should obey God and keep all of His commandments, including the Sabbath of the fourth commandment. Jesus kept and taught it. He commanded His disciples to remember it in their prayers for forty long years after the cross, before Jerusalem fell, that their "flight be not . . . on the sabbath day" (Matt. 24:20).

He inspired the gospel prophet to declare that in the earth made new every saved person will come up and worship God on the Sabbath day (Isa. 66:23). All of Christ's close followers kept the seventh-day Sabbath. Paul consistently kept it and taught it (Acts 17:2). Peter followed Jesus as his example (1 Peter 2:21). John called it "the Lord's day" (Rev. 1:10). So this man and his wife decided to begin keeping the Lord's holy day.

One day the pastor and I paid them a visit. After we talked together for some time, answering many of their questions, we came to the topic of baptism. Neither of them had experienced immersion.

The pastor then remarked, "You may be baptized *if* you are *willing*." But the "if" expressed doubt. And the word "willing" sounded about the same. So I quickly changed the statement into, "I believe you good people have thought about baptism, haven't you?"

"Yes, we have," they smiled.

"And I imagine you have hoped that someday you might be baptized, haven't you?"

159

Again I smiled. And their reply was, "Yes, we have."
"Wonderful," I continued.

Then I made some suggestions concerning efforts that
Satan might make to discourage them. As I spoke I noticed
that they were nodding assent. And I knew I had touched
on some of the very problems they had been pondering,
you see. And yet some members of the local church had
intimated that they were not ready for baptism. This expression of doubt had almost discouraged this lovely young
couple. But these expressions of faith, mixed with love
and courtesy, encouraged them and made them very happy.

We mentioned the fact that there was to be a
baptismal service that very night, and they were welcome
to come and be baptized. We did not ask them if they
were "willing." We spoke faith. We looked faith. We
acted faith.

When we closed our visit with a word of prayer, the
pastor offered one of the best prayers of faith to which I
have ever listened. He did not mention "if" any more.
But he expressed faith in them and their eagerness to
walk with the Lord. It was a beautifully worded prayer in
its aspect of expressed faith.

After we left the home I remarked to the pastor as we
rode along in his car that he was most adept at picking up
this principle of soul winning. He had grasped the difference between doubt and faith in a moment. I want to tell
you, friends, men who can change their philosophy from
one of doubt, of skepticism, to one of faith are needed
everywhere.

The pastor was a young man, but I noticed he was
holding down a large charge. What he did in that home
explained to me his success. He was eager to learn. He was
quick to make changes that would make him more

efficient. May we all be determined not to rest satisfied with our old methods that have not produced a harvest of souls.

FAITH WORKS TODAY

At the close of one of our meetings a fellow minister and I stepped outside the tabernacle. And there stood a young woman. She had been planning on baptism. But now she was all out of the notion. We could see she was almost vexed.

We lifted our hearts to God in prayer as we visited with her. And we began talking faith.

One of us said, "*You* love the Lord."

What do you suppose she replied?

"Yes, I do. Yes, I do."

"I believe you are going to serve Him," continued the other.

Softening a little, she said, "Yes, I am."

This young woman had attended nearly all the meetings, so we knew she had a very good background for understanding the truths of God's Holy Word. So one of us added kindly, "And you really love the Sabbath. I *know* you love it."

"Yes, I do," she replied in more subdued tones.

The other minister climaxed the conversation by saying, "And you are going to keep it, aren't you?"

"Yes, I *am* going to," was her pleasant but firm reply.

This all took place in perhaps three minutes or so! We ministers demonstrated faith. We *talked* faith. We *looked* faith. We *thought* faith. And God rewarded our faith. At no time in our conversation did either of us denounce or judge her by saying, "What's happened to you, you poor stubborn thing!" Oh, no! But rather we affirmed, "You love the Lord. We know you love Him."

11

THE BETTER METHOD

In my early experience in the ministry I thought the way to bring people to a decision was to say to them, point blank, "Now, what are you going to do about it?" But I do not use that method any more. *Now* I endeavor to express *faith* in them. I might begin something like this, "You know, I believe *you* really love the Lord." If another minister is visiting with me, I often say, "Pastor So-and-so, this man truly loves the Lord." And I notice his face brightens. Then perhaps I look at him and say, "You do, don't you?"

"Yes," he will doubtless say, "I really do."

How much better that is than to say to him, "Do you love the Lord?" Why should I raise the question? Why not *help* him to say the right thing? Yes, help him by suggesting, "You love the Lord, don't you?" You see, the devil is trying to make him think he does *not* love the Lord. The *Lord* wants him to believe that he *does*. So *I* want to side with the Lord, don't you? So why not suggest, "*You* love the Lord." Many a soul will respond by saying, "Yes, I do."

You might be surprised, my friends, to know how many people, deep down in their hearts, really love the Lord. They *want* to do what is right. They need to be shown *how* to do it!

Then later, if I have known the person well enough and know that he has gone far enough in the study of the truth, I sometimes say something like: "I want to make a prediction. When anybody loves the Lord as this man (or this woman) does, I just about know what is going to happen to him. I am going to make a prediction, Pastor So-and-so, that one of these days this good man is going to request membership in the church."

162

Of course we would never think of saying anything like that when we *first* know him. No, never! That would be one of the worst things we could do, and would doubtless drive him away altogether. But there *is* a proper time to make such a statement. It may be many months after the person has known the gospel truth. Sometimes I say, "Anyone as honest as this man will never be satisfied in doing less than walking in *all* the light. Isn't that so, brother?"

And he will doubtless reply something like, "Yes, I want to walk in all the light." It often happens just like that. *Of course* he wants to walk in the light. There are *many* people who want to walk in the light. They need encouragement. Sometimes the man starts right in by saying, "I know the seventh day is the Sabbath, but I don't know *how* to keep it."

Now is the time for me to express *real faith* in him, and faith in God. *Now* I must show him *how* to keep the Sabbath. And I *show* him—not *scold* him, not belittle him! But I *show* him the path of faith. I present the simple steps he is to take, and perhaps the very next Sabbath he is in church. He is keeping the Sabbath. That is right! I have experienced it time and again.

FAITH—NOT DOUBT

A young man attended my meetings in a Southern city. With others, he came forward for victory over tobacco. This was on a Thursday evening. Do you suppose I said to him, "Look here, brother, if you can keep the victory over smoking for six weeks, we will baptize you"? Would that have been expressing faith in him? No! Neither would it be expressing faith in God.

Rather I said, "I will explain to you the A B C of victory. A—is Ask, according to a Bible promise (Matt.

7:7). B—is Believe, and tell the Lord you believe (Mark 11:22-24). C—is Claim what He has promised (Rom. 10:10; 1 Cor. 15:57). And right now you can have the victory through Jesus."

It is really very simple. And he believed it all, and put it into practice. He went back home that night and never smoked again.

He was working for a railroad company. At first he was given the Sabbath off, and continued to be employed. Later he was discharged. But this young man believed the promise of God that if he made God first, his living would be "added" (Matt. 6:33). And his wife was as firm in her belief as was her husband. He received a call from another city where he was offered a good job with the Sabbath off. He is receiving about fifty dollars a month *more* than he was receiving before he began to keep the Sabbath. What a reward of faith!

It was on a Thursday night that this young man and his wife came forward for victory and surrender. Sabbath afternoon, two days later, they were baptized. And to the glory of God it can be said that he never went back to his habits of sin. This was accomplished through faith. More than a year later I met this same young couple again in their new church. They were now leaders in the church.

Unquestioning faith that God will surely grant complete victory is essential. Had I expressed doubt in the suggesting of putting him on trial, he might still be a victim of tobacco. He might also be earning fifty dollars less a month. Of course, if a man does not accept victory by faith, he should not be baptized. No, that would not be fair either to him or to God. I do not believe in baptizing people who do not know whether God has given them victory. *No, never!*

Sometimes we Christians are inclined to become dis-

164

couraged if a person does not receive perfect victory when we visit him once or twice. But let us be patient. "Feeling the terrible power of temptation, the drawing desire that leads to indulgence, many a man cries in despair, 'I can not resist evil.' Tell him that he can, that he must resist. He may have been overcome again and again, but it need not be always thus. He is weak in moral power, controlled by the habits of a life of sin. His promises and resolutions are like ropes of sand. The knowledge of his broken promises and forfeited pledges weakens his confidence in his own sincerity, and causes him to feel that God cannot accept him or work with his efforts. But he need not despair."—*The Ministry of Healing,* pp. 174, 175. "You will watch over and encourage them, and your sympathy and confidence will make it hard for them to fall from their steadfastness."—*Christ's Object Lessons,* p. 197. "He [Jesus] honored man with His confidence, and thus placed him on his honor."—*Testimonies to Ministers,* p. 190.

GERTRUDE

Gertrude was a tobacco addict. For twenty-five years she had used it. When the doctor informed her that she must break company with it, she tried. But she could hold out for no longer than five hours, even though she knew the baneful results of continuing.

Other Christians tried to help her. But to no avail. When a series of meetings was begun in Gertrude's city she attended. At an afterservice she expressed her desire for release from tobacco. So we gave her the A B C of victory.

The next morning my wife and I visited her in her home. We celebrated victory with her. We did not ask her if she could stop smoking. We told her she *had*

165

stopped. We smiled. But she groaned. Later she confided in us that she hardly knew how she could have stopped the habit, for she had never been able to do so before. But we had smiled and encouraged her, and let her know that she was *through* with it. We also told her we would return, or have someone else do so, twice each day. And we did. Each visit was a faith visit. It was a victory celebration.

After her first week of complete release (for she has never touched it again—the last we heard) she remarked, "Had you told me I *had* to stop smoking, I could not have done it, but you simply put me in the arms of Jesus." And we had also put around her arms of faith and love.

We did, however, tell her that if she smoked again, it would doubtless be seven times harder to quit than it was this time. But that would be the only difference, for we would never cease to be her friends. We knew she had victory. And she did. She was baptized less than two weeks later.

THE PROBLEM CHILD

"I'm going to quit," thought a schoolteacher to herself. She was having a hard time. "What's the use of working for these youngsters?" One boy in particular was very hard to get along with. He was the ringleader of troublesome boys. So as she was walking home to lunch on this particular day she was thinking, "Yes, I'm going to quit!"

But even as these thoughts were passing through her mind, she realized that one of her biggest "problems" was walking right along beside her. It was this "ringleader." They began chatting together. As they came to the fork in the road where their ways parted, the "incorrigible" said to her, "Teacher, ma'am, if you was me, when you grew up, what would you be?"

166

"I never believed *that* boy had enough sense even to think of what he might be when he became a man. What! He actually has a serious thought!" she was thinking fast to herself.

But she succeeded in concealing her surprise as she calmly answered, "What had you thought of becoming when you grow up?"

"Well," replied the boy, "ma'am, if you think I could be, I'd like to be a doctor."

Again she tried to hide her shock as she replied very interestedly, "That would be fine! Yes, I believe that would be all right."

"Do you think I could be, ma'am?" queried the boy, seeking assurance from his teacher.

"Well, y-e-s," came from her lips slowly, for there was nothing else she could say. "Why, yes, I believe you could."

"All right, ma'am. Then I'll try to be a doctor," he answered with some finality in his tone.

With that they parted. Each went home to lunch. But the teacher could hardly eat. Her mind was on that conversation with her "incorrigible" pupil.

As she returned to the schoolroom after lunch hour it was with a new resolve. She would continue teaching! She would help that boy to become the doctor he wanted to be. She would help the other pupils also. And so she continued to fulfill her mission of teaching. That particular boy had been a D student. But after that conversation with his teacher his grades picked up. And he was graduated from grammar school with honors.

He entered high school. His teacher kept in touch with him, encouraging him and expressing confidence in him. Then he went on to college. The grammar-school teacher by this time was married. But when the boy was graduated from college she was there, sitting on the front row. And after the graduation exercises were over the young man walked down to his former teacher and exclaimed warmly, "I owe it to you. It was the confidence you expressed in me that helped me make the grade."

Then he was accepted in the school of medicine. In the meantime there was born into the home of the teacher a sweet little boy. A few years passed. Her little treasure became seriously ill. The doctors held out no hope.

At this critical moment a young doctor stepped into the home. "By God's help, I think I can spare that boy to you," spoke the young physician comfortingly to the grief-stricken parents. He stood by the bedside and felt the pulse of the sick lad. "I can perform an operation, and I believe he will pull through," he said assuringly.

"All right, doctor, do what you can," replied the tearful mother.

The young doctor performed the delicate operation. He put the boy in bed and stayed by his side until he could look into the face of the mother and say, "Your little one is out of danger."

And who was that successful young surgeon? He was the "incorrigible" boy of yesterday of that grammar school. But the words of faith and confidence his teacher had expressed in him during those trying days, set his feet in the path to success. Faith pays *big* dividends.

FAITH OF JESUS

"This is the victory that overcometh the world, even our faith" (1 John 5:4). It was faith that inspired even Jesus in His hour of trial. "He shall see of the travail of his soul, and shall be satisfied" (Isa. 53:11). By faith Jesus saw the reward of His suffering, a host of saved men and women, boys and girls.

When Jesus comes again, those who are saved are to have the "faith of Jesus" (Rev. 14:12). Their *doctrines* will be full of *faith*. Their *prayers* will be *mixed* with *faith*. Their *lives* will be aflame with *faith*. They will believe in God. They will have had confidence in their fellow man. It takes this faith to make it possible for God's grace to be operative. And it is this faith that builds up hope in the sinner's heart.

It is amazing, the results that follow wherever loving faith is used to win souls. "The Lord Jesus is making experiments on human hearts through the exhibition of His mercy and abundant grace. He is effecting transformations so amazing that Satan, with all his triumphant boasting, with all his confederacy of evil united against God and the laws of His government, stands viewing them as a fortress impregnable to his sophistries and delusions. They are to him an incomprehensible mystery. The angels of God . . . look on with astonishment and joy, that fallen men, once children of wrath, are through the training of Christ developing characters after the divine similitude, to be sons and daughters of God, to act an important part in the occupations and pleasures of heaven." —*Ibid.*, p. 18.

I hope you catch the picture. Here is a sinner. He was once so weak that he was like a reed shaken in the wind. The devil could get him to do anything he wished. Now, through the grace of Jesus, Satan sees him no longer a wavering, vacillating man, but a fortress impregnable. Satan cannot understand it. He and his angels look on and exclaim, "This is an incomprehensible mystery! We cannot understand it! We cannot budge him from the right any more. Yet once he was such an easy victim."

God knows what made the difference. The change came by the silent working of the Holy Spirit, through the grace of God, upon his heart. "Angels of God . . . look on with astonishment and joy." They see one who was once a child of wrath, the plaything of the devil, now prepared to act an important part in the pleasures and occupations of heaven.

IT WILL LIGHT THEM HOME

I read of a preacher living in town who was visiting some backwoods settlers. By the time he was ready to return home it was very dark. One of the settlers gave the preacher a torch of pitch-pine wood to light his way along the dark road toward home. The preacher had never before seen anything like it, and remarked, "It will soon burn out."

"It will light you home," replied the woodsman.

"But the wind may blow it out," remonstrated the preacher.

"It will light you home," repeated his new friend.

"But what if it should rain?" he still questioned.

"It will light you home," was the insistent reply.

And faith is the light. The Chinese have a proverb, "Don't curse the darkness; light a candle." So where we have in the past belittled or condemned the wrongdoer, let us switch to the philosophy of expressing confidence in what he may become through the grace of God. One philosophy is doubt. The other is faith. One fails, the other succeeds. This expressed faith is Christ's successful method. We may be successful, too, in showing many a lost sinner the way back to our Father's house by expressions of faith.

Jesus Loves

~~~~~~

*S*HE HAS the long, slender fingers of an artist, beautiful brown eyes, a pretty, pointed nose, black hair, and a complexion unmarred by rouge or lipstick." So reported a radio commentator. He was describing the Parisian girl who is working on her Ph.D. by writing a book describing the typical Parisian woman. But it is impossible to describe the love of Jesus Christ. We can only point out some of the characteristics of His love, which show it to be altogether different from "love" as we commonly know it.

HUMBLE LOVE

"Oh, we love him!" was the exclamation of a man and his wife who held bitter feelings toward a brother in the church.

"Could you go to him and put your arms around him?" I inquired.

"We! Put our arms around *him!*" came back the retort. And then they proceeded to denounce the very man they had professed to love. They pictured themselves as above him in honesty, decency, purity, and fairness.

Yet the Scriptures command us to "let this mind be

171

in you, which was also in Christ Jesus: who, being in the form of God, thought it not robbery to be equal with God: but made himself of no reputation, and took upon him the form of a servant, and was made in the likeness of men: and being found in fashion as a man, he humbled himself, and became obedient unto death, even the death of the cross" (Phil. 2:5-8). *That* is the love of Jesus. It is first of all *humble* love. Love does not climb on stilts. It does not act superior. It is meek. It is lowly.

Jesus had an entirely different concept of love from that of the religious leaders of His day. He said to them, "Ye are they which justify yourselves before men" (Luke 16:15). "I dwell," He declares, "with him . . . that is of a contrite and humble spirit" (Isa. 57:15).

Webster's dictionary gives one definition of "humble" as "to bring down; to reduce to a low state." Christ reduced Himself to a low estate. He did not become worried when someone else tried to reduce Him. He had already reduced Himself, because it was necessary to do so in order to save us. Then He commands us, "Learn of me; for I am meek and lowly in heart" (Matt. 11:28-30).

CHANGE TO HUMILITY

Then in winning souls, I have the first key of love from Christ. It is *humble* love. That means that I am not to take an attitude of superiority, either in intellect or spirituality, over the one whom I seek to win to Christ. "Let each esteem other better than themselves," is the key (Phil. 2:3). I had been preaching for many years before I ever thought of love as being connected with humility. But there is no true love that is not humble.

Mrs. Brink came to me weeping. She had a daughter for whom she was burdened. But in spite of her scoldings, her threatenings, her severity, the girl did not yield to her mother's wishes or standards. We had just concluded a study on soul winning.

"What shall I do?" wept Mrs. Brink.

"I would suggest that you follow the instructions that I gave just a few moments ago in our study," I carefully and kindly pointed out to her. In those instructions I had mentioned how I, too, had made mistakes in my methods of soul winning. I had thought I was representing Christ's love. But I had not connected humility with love. Consequently I had not reflected true love at all.

Mrs. Brink sadly, but in a determined way, exclaimed, almost in a whisper, "That is just what I am going to do!" But I could see she wanted a bit more advice on how to begin.

"To clear the slate," I began, "I have found it necessary to apologize. If I were in your place, I would return home, call my daughter to me and say, 'Honey, I want you to please forgive me for the way I have treated you. I will never scold or condemn you again, by the grace of God.'"

The preacher attitude, the teacher attitude, the professor attitude, is not the loving attitude. It will never do in the field of soul winning. Souls are won only by individuals who come down to the plane of those for whom they labor. We cannot tell a sinner he is doing right. Oh, no! That would be untrue. God has already made clear that "all have sinned" (Rom. 3:23). But we can state to the sinner that we also are sinners, and perhaps bigger ones in the sight of God than any for whom we labor. Our greater light makes our sin more heinous. The savage of the jungle may not be as guilty before God as a sinning Christian. So we have *all* sinned.

Jesus took humanity. This made it possible for us to talk with Him without being stricken down by His glory.

Jesus often referred to Himself as the Son of *man*. This was because it was absolutely essential for Him to humble Himself in order to save us. Otherwise we would be afraid to confide in Him. If *Jesus* did it, then *we* must also. This is love—*humble* love. The apostle Paul agrees with this when he states that love "seeketh not her own" (1 Cor. 13:5). Oh, how we need *humble* love!

PROOF OF BIRTH

For the sake of illustration, imagine a child who is in this world several months before he knows he has been born. And then one day he sees some pink things moving in front of his face. One of them gets into his mouth. And his little jaws come down on the finger. And it then dawns upon him that these pink things belong to him, and that he has been born.

God tells us that we can know that we are born again. "Every one that loveth is born of God" (1 John 4:7). But loving only my friends is not true humble love. "Love your enemies" (Matt. 5:44) is Jesus' command. Even the publicans saluted those who were friendly to them. But only he who is a Christian can love and bless those who talk against him. That is *humble* love. And anything that falls short of that is not real love.

LOVING-KINDNESS

God says, "With lovingkindness have I drawn thee" (Jer. 31:3). "If there is a God, I demand that He strike me down instantly," cried an infidel defiantly. And just then a scrap of paper was blown to the ground at his feet. Only three words appeared on the paper. They were, "God is love." What a wonderful Saviour!

"For he is kind unto the unthankful and to the evil" (Luke 6:35), said Jesus. He was explaining that being "perfect, even as your Father which is in heaven is perfect" (Matt. 5:48), means: "Be ye therefore merciful, as your Father also is merciful" (Luke 6:36). So love is interpreted as being merciful, or kind.

Perfection in soul winning, then, consists of being *kind,* or merciful, to evil people. One of the definitions of "kind" that Webster gives will doubtless be as revealing to you as it was to me: "Of a gentle and teachable disposition, as a horse in harness or under the saddle." To be kind as a soul winner means that we will listen to others. We will not be dogmatic or arbitrary. We will respect others' ideas, others' views, others' interpretation of Scripture. "Kindness" is only a shade from "humility" in its passive aspect. But in its active aspect it relieves distress, comforts the sorrowing, brings hope to the erring.

It is, therefore, impossible for a man to be kind unless he is humble. And it is impossible to prove his kindness unless it is demonstrated to those who are undeserving, evil, unthankful.

CHANGING TO HUMBLE LOVE

Sister Holier-than-thou attended a complete series of revival meetings. To all appearances she was a wonderful Christian. As I recall now, she was a leading officer in her church. But Mrs. Holier-than-thou had a brother who felt that she had done him an injustice. So he had absented himself from church for a long time. Of course this shows that he was slipping back. There is no question about that. One with a progressive Christian experience will not refrain from going to church merely because he thinks someone has been unfair to him. He attends church to help others, as well as to receive a blessing himself. So there is no question but that this brother had taken the wrong attitude. He was wandering far from God.

175

But Mrs. Holier-than-thou knew about this. She knew that there was something her brother held against her. But she came to the revival meetings just the same.

Then one day it dawned over Mrs. Holier-than-thou that "if thou bring thy gift to the altar, and there rememberest that thy brother hath ought against thee; leave there thy gift before the altar, and go thy way; first be reconciled to thy brother, and then come and offer thy gift" (Matt. 5:23, 24).

Mrs. Holier-than-thou came to the conclusion that the best way possible to win her brother back to Christ was by being kind to him, going over to his home, humbling herself before him in a sincere apology. And so that is what she did. Then she changed from being Mrs. Holier-than-thou to Mrs. Humble. She was kind to her backslidden brother instead of being neglectful of his feelings. I tell you, my friends, there is a lot of soul-winning material in a humble and kind Christian. Downright humility goes a long way in winning our relatives and friends to Jesus.

The word "courteous" is used just once in the Scriptures. "Love as brethren, be pitiful, be courteous" (1 Peter 3:8). I am not a Greek scholar, but the word from which "courteous" is translated, Dr. Young states, is *philophron.* Sounds as though it had a root similar to "Philadelphia," meaning "brotherly love." So courtesy is one avenue by which love expresses itself.

Jesus treated Judas, His traitor, with *philophron.* He washed his feet. He called him "friend."

Love, then, precludes strife. "The servant of the Lord must not strive" (2 Tim. 2:24). In giving help to sinners, "one drop of gall in it will be poison to the hearer or the reader. Because of that drop of poison, one will discard all your good and acceptable words."—*Gospel Workers,* p. 375.

176

Courteous Love

I walked into a Baptist Bible class one day. As I stepped inside the door, a gentleman reached out and took my hand, shook it warmly as he smiled graciously, and said, "I am glad to welcome you." Oh, that made me feel *so* good. But it was not enough for him merely to shake my hand, and with his other hand he reached up and took hold of my elbow, as he smiled again and gave me a little pat of appreciation. Oh, that was courteous love. As this gracious, courteous man was ushering me to my seat, we passed another man who bowed and greeted me.

I like to see courteous love, don't you? I like people to step right up to the stranger as he enters the sanctuary and greet him with gracious courtesy. And when you receive *that* kind of reception, you feel that love is all around you. Hearts open wide to the Spirit of Jesus.

As the teacher of this Baptist Sunday school class rose before his class, he took time to recognize me. He said, "How do you do?" He took time to shake my hand. I don't suppose that *all* Baptist or *all* Methodist Sunday school teachers do that. And I don't believe *all* Adventist Sabbath school teachers do that, either. But you know, I have an idea, from what I have been studying, that it is more important for me to greet the stranger in my Sabbath school class than it is to take that extra time on the study of the lesson. I would rather take only half the time allotted to the class period, if necessary, in the study of the lesson and use the other half in being courteous and kind to the strangers in my class, giving them a warm welcome, than to leave them unrecognized. I would introduce the guests to the members of the class and say, "We are happy to have you meet these good folks." You see, friends, courtesy helps people to come to Jesus.

12

"I'm Mad at You"

In my early ministry I was assistant to a pastor in Washington, D.C. I well remember an experience he had with one of his parishioners. One day he called on her in her home. She greeted him at the door with, "I'm mad at you."

Keen witted as he was, he replied, "I am mad at you too."

"What are you mad at me for?" she asked in amazement.

"Well, you tell me first why you are mad at me," returned her preacher.

"I'm mad at you because you did not shake hands with me last Sabbath."

"And that is just why I am mad at you," he replied with a hearty laugh. And then of course they both laughed. But from that time on that fine woman realized that she was an *assistant* to the pastor, and not a patient in a hospital. As a church member it was her duty to welcome everyone, even the pastor, who at the moment might have his mind on something else and accidentally overlook her.

Every church should have a welcoming committee. Every stranger should be warmly welcomed and made to feel at home. But more than this, every Christian should be a welcoming committee all on his own. We should not wait for someone else to welcome the friends, the guests, and the strangers. We all should do it. It may mean everything to some heavyhearted soul. This is courteous love.

Tenderhearted Love

At home in the evening, when we gathered around the circle for family worship, it was father's custom to apologize to us boys if he had been impatient with us during the day. One day father had been harsh and unkind to me. When evening came he either forgot or neglected to apologize to me. Discouraged, heavyhearted, and hurt, I went upstairs to my room. I climbed into bed, turned my face toward the wall, and cried like a little boy can. I even used some pretty big words to myself in describing my father. Of course father did not know how I felt. I never would have dared to answer him back or speak unkindly of him in his hearing at any time. But there all alone I very easily found words at my command. I was calling my father a hypocrite. I was thinking, "He can preach all he wants to in church, but I have no confidence in *his* religion. When I grow up, I'll have nothing to do with it."

And just then I heard someone touch the latch on the stairway door. Then I heard father's step coming up the stairway. I tried to make believe I was asleep. But in a moment I felt a face down close to mine. And I heard a voice in deep humility saying, "Son, will you forgive me for being impatient with you today?"

Immediately father became to me a hero! And why the change in my feeling toward him? Because he was big enough to apologize to me.

But friends, we must not wait for others to apologize to us before we have the spirit of forgiveness. We are to be "tenderhearted, forgiving one another, even as God for Christ's sake hath forgiven you" (Eph. 4:32). Then God can use us to win men to Christ.

And that is love. It is to be tenderhearted, not hardhearted. We must not entertain hard feelings. It is His wonderful, *tender* love that draws us to Christ, "because he first loved us" (1 John 4:19). Jesus not merely cries out in behalf of His enemies, "Father, forgive them" (Luke 23:34) but He promises, "though your sins be as scarlet, they shall be as white as snow" (Isa. 1:18). And it is He who has taught us to pray, "Forgive us our debts, *as* we forgive our debtors" (Matt. 6:12). That is real love. To be tenderhearted means that we do not hold hard feelings toward anyone. That is being like Jesus. And "he that loveth not knoweth not God; for God is love" (1 John 4:8). Love "thinketh no evil" (1 Cor. 13:5).

PITIFUL LOVE

Jesus loved us when we were yet sinners. He loved us when we were enemies of His. He came down to earth and lived and died for us (Rom. 5:8-10). Isaiah describes us as having "wounds, and bruises, and putrifying sores" (Isa. 1:5, 6). But Jesus, the Great Physician, came and healed us. Our best garments are only filthy rags in the sight of God (Isa. 64:6). But Jesus came and gave us a new dress. We "were dead in trespasses and sins" (Eph. 2:1), but He brought us to life.

Imagine, if you can, someone standing beside a casket. Lying in that casket is a very unlovely person dressed in rags. The one gazing into the bier says with all sincerity, "I love that person—not with a love that pities merely, but with a love that marries."

Did you ever hear of such love as that? And yet, *that* is the love of Jesus Christ for you and for me. This is "loving-kindness." It is humble love. It is courtesy in action. God is tenderhearted. He is pitiful. He is all of this, and infinitely more. His is the mysterious love that longs to marry such a despicable individual (Jeremiah 3). I cannot understand it. I cannot comprehend it. It is a "great mystery" (Eph. 5:32). It is God's great love for you and for me.

And now *I* love *Him.* In so doing I am merely responding to His love. "We love him, because he first loved us" (1 John 4:19). We are not worthy of His love. We *know* that. But He was so kind to us when we were mean and ugly! We were enemies, and so unlovely, dressed in rags, and filthy garments, all covered with spiritual sores! He loved us in spite of it all. What kindness! What pity!

That is why *I* love Him so. Isn't that why *you* love Him? He did not condemn me. "For God sent not his Son into the world to condemn the world" (John 3:17). He did not judge me. Though "the wages of sin is death" (Rom. 6:23), yet He came to save me. "Thou shalt call his name JESUS: for he shall save his people from their sins" (Matt. 1:21). He did not come to leave me in that awful condition in which He found me. "If any man be in Christ, he is a new creature" (2 Cor. 5:17). Thank God for the wonderful, pitying, tenderhearted love of Jesus!

Having come to Jesus, having been recipients of His matchless love, we are invited to carry to others the wonderful love of our Saviour. Thus we win them to Christ. And "he that winneth souls is wise" (Prov. 11:30).

Since I have learned how Jesus won me, I can use the same methods to win someone else to Him. I don't have to argue. I don't have to condemn. I don't have to judge. But I can reveal the simple, wholesome love of Jesus. Others will thus be won to Him.

A Mighty Challenge

There are five simple Christian graces, which, when employed, will bring a hundred to Jesus where we are now bringing one. (*Testimonies,* vol. 9, p. 189.) Isn't that wonderful! If I can learn what it is that is keeping men and women from accepting Jesus Christ, and then if I can learn how I can bring a hundred to the Master where now I win but one, I would like to cease to do the things that are keeping them out, and do the five simple things that will bring them in. Wouldn't you? I believe you would.

It would pay us to have several church board meetings just to take time to consider those five graces. We could

181

study carefully, then kneel before God and say, "Lord, help us to learn those five essentials. If we can learn them, we can have a hundred conversions where we now have one!" That would be worth having a business meeting of the whole church, and spending the entire time in studying these five points! Why, if we could discover a way by which a hundred would be won to Christ where now there is only one, it would be worth having many conventions to learn the secret, wouldn't it? It would well pay us to put on a conference-wide program to learn those five essentials. It would be time well spent to gather together the ministers, the Bible instructors, the laymen, and learn what those five features are, and how to put them into practice. We could then win *a hundred* souls to Christ where now we are winning but *one*.

It would pay to spend thousands of dollars, if necessary, in learning this great secret! Twice as much money as we are now expending would be good economy if we could thereby learn how to win one hundred where we now win one. If we spent twice as much money as we are now, and yet won a hundred souls to Christ where now we are winning one, it would be the greatest investment we have ever made. Isn't that true?

If we should go so far as to spend *ten times* as much money as we are now spending, and by so doing succeed in learning those *five* graces that would bring to Christ one hundred times as many souls as we are now bringing, it would still be the most glorious investment this cause has ever made!

It ought, then, to be a campaign—a conference-wide campaign, a union-wide campaign, a denominational-wide campaign, a world-wide campaign. It would be worth all the extra money invested if we could win a hundred to the Lord Jesus Christ where we now win one. We ought to develop a great program revolving around those five essentials. And yet, so far as I can see, *no* additional expense is necessary. This fact is challenging. We need merely a changed program, a new philosophy, such as Christ used. Let us learn what these five essentials are.

A great soul winner once wrote, "The Lord does not now work to bring many souls into the truth, because——" Let us pause here a moment. The reason many more in the world are not coming to Jesus is either their hardness or something wrong with us. "The Lord does not now work to bring many souls into the truth, because of the church members."—*Ibid.,* vol. 6, p. 371. Then *I* am a liability to God instead of an asset unless I use His methods. Isn't that right? Since there are *a hundred* around us waiting to come in while we are bringing *one* to Christ, it cannot be because they are hard. No, there is another reason for this lack. It is because of professed Christians who are not converted to Christ's methods. It is because of unconverted church members, using unconverted methods. It is because of backslidden church members using backslidden methods.

Here, then, are the five essentials we have been talking about. See how simple they are! And let us remember that if we would develop these five graces, there would be a hundred conversions where now there is but one. "If we would humble ourselves before God, and be kind and courteous and tender-hearted and pitiful, there would be one hundred conversions to the truth where now there is only one."—*Ibid.,* vol. 9, p. 189.

1. Humble ourselves before God.
2. Be kind.
3. Be courteous.
4. Be tenderhearted.
5. Be pitiful.

We should not be less agressive in our study of Bible doctrine. We should accelerate our pace. We should multiply our efforts in literature distribution. More and more should evangelism fill our lives. We should be able to give Bible proof for our every position. But the preaching of doctrine must be given proper balance. "And now abideth faith, hope, charity, these three; but the greatest of these is charity" (1 Cor. 13:13). *Love, faith,* and *hope*—all-enduring principles—can never take second place to any other doctrine. They are eternal. And we neglect them only at the peril of some soul.

LOVE THEM IN

Do you know, my friends, the world is lonesome? People in the world long to know that somebody loves them with a love that is humble, and kind, and pitiful, and tenderhearted. They are desperately lonesome, friends. You don't know how extremely lonesome people are unless *you* have been lonesome. No ordinary love will meet the needs of lost humanity. Only the love of Jesus will do.

In a revival held some time ago a woman responded to the invitation to come to the altar in token of a surrendered life to the Master. This was only the second Sabbath morning she had ever been in an Adventist church. In the invitation I had included all those who would like to join the Sabbathkeeping church. This good woman had been studying one of the Bible correspondence courses. She had come to the conclusion that the seventh day is the right day to keep, and had determined to keep it. She was in harmony with all the other Bible doctrines as well. So she wanted to join the Seventh-day Adventist Church.

But you know, friends, she was *awfully* lonesome. Her children had no room for her. So she was in a rooming house alone in a strange city. She was already a Christian,

184

but had found a little more light in the teachings of the Adventist Church. She wanted to walk in the added light. And so it is with a Christian—he always desires to walk in more light as it comes to him.

So as I extended the invitation that Sabbath morning this woman came forward. That morning I had been talking about the love of Jesus. This dear woman confided later: "You know, as I came forward in response to your invitation, and was standing there all alone, I said in my heart, 'Lord, I wish somebody would love me.' I had no sooner poured out my heart to the Lord than Mrs. Coon stepped up by my side and put her arm around me." She was so surprised and happy that she turned right there and kissed my wife on the cheek. That dear soul had been *so* lonesome, and that little act of my wife meant more to her than many sermons might have. She needed humble, courteous, tenderhearted, pitying love. Nothing less would have answered her need.

Sitting in the congregation that same morning was a man who I later learned had been married to an Adventist for more than thirty years. But he was not a professing Christian. Later he told me, "When you were preaching that Sabbath morning you preached a regular old Methodist sermon. And I felt the Lord calling me." Then he added, "You preached right at me."

"Oh, no, I wasn't preaching at you," I remonstrated. "It must have been the Lord's Spirit speaking to your heart, for I thought you were already a Christian."

At the close of the service that morning he too responded to the invitation to surrender his life to the Master and take his stand with the Sabbathkeeping church. Passing this man as she was leaving the church, my wife stepped over to him, shook his hand warmly, and said, "God bless you."

But he expressed to her his feeling of utter weakness and helplessness. He had taken his stand for Christ, but felt his extreme weakness and questioned his ability to hold out. My wife assured him, "God will see you through. He will *never* fail you."

Later as I visited this fine man in his home he said to me, "I hardly know which helped me the most—your sermon or your wife's speaking to me after the service. That meant *so* much to me."

The world is lonesome, friends. The world is dying for a little bit of love. Soul winning is a love affair. There is no question about that. In order to bring people to Jesus we must *love* them to Jesus. When they step into the vestibule of any of our churches they must find someone there with a warm, loving handshake to welcome them. This is courteous love. When they leave the assembly of God's children it must be the same. Everyone should be shaking the hand of someone else. Why? Because the world is lonesome, *very* lonesome. And sin has made people more lonesome and more sensitive. So, many times when they enter a Sabbath school class they are lonesome. When they come to church they are lonesome. Wherever we meet them they are in need of love, of kindness, of pity.

Some time ago a man wrote me a long letter. In it he said, "I went to a church. I attended there for six months, but nobody welcomed me. I went into a Sabbath school class. And I attended there for six months. But during that whole time no one introduced me to the class. Nobody shook my hand and said, 'I'm glad you are here.'"

Then he said to me, "Will you tell the people to go to the stranger in their midst, shake his hand, and make him feel welcome and at home?" And he continued, "I felt as though the text of scripture was almost fulfilled that says, 'No man cared for my soul.'" He was at that very time passing through great trouble. And he said, "It seemed that in the very church where I was worshiping week after week no one cared for my soul."

Friends, let that *never* again be said of any of us. Let it never be said! Let us demonstrate a courteous love, a humble love, a tenderhearted love.

Someone *does* care for our souls. It is Jesus. And "we love him, because he first loved us" (1 John 4:19). Let us ever remember that all around us there are dear ones whose hearts are pressed down like an ox under its burden. They are praying and pleading for help, for love, for pity, for tenderness, for kindness. They are praying for somebody, *somebody* to love them. They are longing for someone to reach out a hand of humble, understanding love.

LOVE IN ACTION

When I was a lad I heard a minister tell the story of a soldier boy dying on the battlefield. The chaplain, Bible in hand, found him lying there on the cold ground. He wanted to read to the poor boy from the Bible.

"But," said the poor boy to the chaplain, "can you straighten out my neck? It's so cramped." The chaplain ran over, removed a garment from a soldier already dead, rolled it up, and gently straightened the poor boy's cramped neck and placed his head on the pillow to rest.

"I'm so thirsty," the boy continued. The chaplain reached for a canteen from the side of a soldier who would never need it again, tenderly raised the head of the dying lad, and gave him to drink.

"Chaplain, I'm so cold," the boy said again. And once again the chaplain ran, took a coat from a dead soldier, and with fatherly tenderness tucked it around the shivering lad.

187

Then the boy looked up into the face of the chaplain and said, "Mister, if there is anything in the Book that will tell me what makes you so kind to me, read it to me."

The world is cold. Sinners need someone to place around them the warm garments of Jesus. The world is thirsty. The sinner needs someone to press to his parched lips the water of salvation. The world is all mixed up, cramped, confused, frustrated. There is need for someone to say, "Come unto me, . . . and I will give you rest" (Matt. 11:28-30). Will *you* be the one to pass on to some weary, sin-sick soul that wonderful invitation of Jesus? Will you reveal a humble charity, a kind love, a courteous allurement?

This is such a simple thing to do that most Christians look beyond it. So many Christians seem to think that if they can out-argue the sinner, or condemn him a bit, or nag him, or scold him, that will make him a Christian. But oh, no! *That* will *never* do it. We must humble ourselves before God. Then we must ask God to make us courteous Christians, tenderhearted, meek, and lowly followers of the Master. Only Christ can make us kind, and courteous, tenderhearted, and pitiful. Then there are a hundred souls out there in the dark and the cold who will come to Jesus, where now we are winning only one. They will come just as surely as we reflect the fivefold love of Jesus.

If soul winning is that simple, I believe we ought to have a church board meeting and pray about it, don't you? We should say, "God, send us out with those five graces. We ought to have a whole business meeting dedicated to the study of the simplicity of Jesus. Our lay workers, as they go out to work for souls, ought to be tutored in those five essentials. Otherwise we might be unkind. Some soul that is lonely, weary, discouraged, blue, needs a kind word to help him get started again.

And what a privilege is ours to be "workers together with him" (2 Cor. 6:1), using the same methods to win our friends and loved ones as Jesus used to win us. And remember, "with lovingkindness have I drawn thee" (Jer. 31:3).

CAUTION

We must remember that there are two extremes to be avoided. So right here we would like to give a caution. There are safeguards we must place around our soul winning. These are very important. We have learned that soul winning is a love affair. We know that it is absolutely impossible to win anyone to Christ except through love. Augment that with such qualities as faith and hope, and we can win a soul to Christ. Every soul who has ever been won to Christ has been won because of love. "We love him, because he first loved us."

Therefore, since soul winning is a love affair, we must be careful and guarded. As a rule men should work for men, and women for women. Of course there are exceptions, but this should be the general rule. A husband and his wife can work for anyone. My wife and I have often visited women together. After we have chatted concerning the problem, we have knelt and prayed. We have never had an understanding with each other as to what my wife shall do. But as we have arisen, my wife has often stepped over to that women and put her arm around her. Such a gesture is not put on. It just comes from her heart. As she embraces her there may be tears in her eyes. The woman responds with an embrace of appreciation. My wife embraces that woman for both herself and me. She *needs* love. She craves love. It is expected. But it is not for me to throw my arms around her. That is my wife's place.

My friends, soul winning is loving people. So let us

place safeguards around it. "We love him, because he first loved us" (1 John 4:19).

CHESTER GALETTE

When I was but a little boy I heard how Chester Galette drowned Grace Brown, his fiancée, in the Auburn Lake. All his relatives thought he was innocent of the charge of murder. But as they sat in the courtroom and heard the evidence pile up against him, they began to shudder. Then they also became convinced that their own Chester was a murderer.

At the close of the court session the father is said to have made his way over to where his son was sitting in the courtroom. With him was Chester's brother. The father and the brother, in angry denunciation, proceeded to shake their fists in the face of Chester, and disown him. They wanted everyone in the courtroom to know that they were not a party to his nefarious crime against God and society. Still angry, humiliated, and brokenhearted, they left Chester with his guards.

But Chester's little mother was there also. When the father and the brother had finished disowning the boy, his mother made her way through the milling courtroom over to where Chester still sat. She placed a loving arm around him, and a tender, tear-stained cheek against his criminal one. With the hot tears freely flowing down her pale face, she told Chester of her love for him, no matter what the future held in store for him. She told her wayward son how she had loved him as a child, as a youth, as a young man. And now she would never, never fail him. She would love him even unto death.

Nineteen centuries ago the human race seemed hopelessly doomed to eternal ruin. Even the most religious leaders drew their skirts of self-righteousness close about them, admitting there was no hope for most of mankind. The hosts of darkness only denounced and incriminated us for acting so much like him who led us into evil and degradation.

Then Jesus, the matchless Lover, made His way to our darkened planet. He was clothed in the humblest garments of humanity, but fragrant with heaven's alabaster box of humility, tenderness, kindness, and pitying courtesy. He placed His matchless arms of love around our criminal forms, and pressed His cheek of pardon close to ours, flushed with sin and evil, and whispered into our ears, now dull of hearing, the words, "Yea, I have loved thee with an everlasting love: therefore with lovingkindness have I drawn thee" (Jer. 31:3). "Come unto me, . . . and I will give you rest" (Matt. 11:28-30).

With a philosophy that cut across that of the religious Pharisaism of His day, and ours, He climaxed His life of love by spreading His hands on the cross of Calvary, while from the heights of Golgotha His penetrating cry entered the very courts of heaven, "Father, forgive them; for they know not what they do" (Luke 23:34).

And from the elevation of the cross we hear Him speak to us, "Go out and share My reconciling love, My heavenly sympathy, My pardoning grace, with those who are unkind, rude, and rebellious." "And all things are of God, who hath reconciled us to himself by Jesus Christ, and hath given to us the ministry of reconciliation; to wit, that God was in Christ, reconciling the world unto himself, not imputing their trespasses unto them; and hath committed unto us the word of reconciliation" (2 Cor. 5:18, 19).